CONTENTS

Our choice:

INTRODUCTION

Time for Food guides are designed to help you find interesting and enjoyable places to eat in the world's main tourist destinations. Each guide divides the destination into eight areas. Each area has a map, followed by a selection of the restaurants, cafés, bars, pubs and food markets in that area. The aim is to cover the whole spectrum of food establishments, from gourmet temples to humble cafés, plus good food shops or delicatessens where you can buy picnic ingredients or food to cook yourself.

If you are looking for a particular restaurant, regardless of its location, or a particular type of cuisine, you can turn to the Food Finder, starting on page 4. This lists all the establishments reviewed in this guide by name (in alphabetical order) and then by cuisine type.

PRICES

Unlike some guides, we have not wasted space telling you how bad a restaurant is – bad or poor-value restaurants simply do not make it into the guide. Many other guides ask restaurants to pay for their entries, or expect the restaurant to advertise in return for a listing. We do neither of these things: the restaurants and cafés

▲ Karlskirche

featured here simply represent a selection of places that the author has sampled and enjoyed.

If there is one consistent criterion for inclusion in the guide, it is good value. Good value does not, of course, necessarily mean cheap. Food lovers know the difference between a restaurant where the high prices are fully justified by the quality of the ingredients and the excellence of the cooking and presentation of the food, and meretricious establishments where high prices are merely the result of pretentious attitudes.

Some of the restaurants featured here are undeniably expensive if you consume caviar and champagne, but even haute cuisine establishments offer set-price menus (especially at lunchtime) allowing budget diners to enjoy dishes created by top chefs and every bit as good as those on the regular menu. At the same time, some of the eating places listed here might not make it into more conventional food guides, because they are relatively humble cafés or takeaways. Some are deliberately oriented towards tourists, but there is nothing wrong in that: what some guides dismiss as 'tourist traps' may be deservedly popular for providing choice and good value.

FEEDBACK

You may or may not agree with the author's choice – in either case we would like to know about your experiences. Any feedback you give us and any recommendations you make will be followed up, so that you can look forward to seeing your restaurant suggestions in print in the next edition.

Feedback forms have been included at the back of the book and you can e-mail us with comments by writing to: *timeforfood@thomascook.com*. Let us know what you like or do not like about the restaurants featured here. Tell us if you discover shops, pubs, cafés, bars, restaurants or markets that

you think should go in the guide. No food guide can keep pace with the changing restaurant scene, as chefs move on, establishments open or close, and menus, opening hours or credit card details change. Let us know if you discover changes – say to telephone numbers or opening times.

Symbols used in this guide

	Visa accepted
	Diners Club accepted
	MasterCard accepted
	Restaurant
	Bar, café or pub
	Shop, market or picnic site
	Telephone
	Transport
②	Numbered red circles relate to the maps at the start of the section

The price indications used in this guide have the following meanings:

●	budget level
●●	typical/average for the destination
●●●	up-market

FOOD FINDER

▲ Naschmarkt

FRENCH
Altwienerhof 66
Le Ciel 66
Hotel im Palais
    Schwarzenberg 67
Saint Michel 10

FUSION
Barbaro's 19

GREEK
Achilleus 48
Artemis 48
Orpheus 20

HUNGARIAN
Gulaschmuseum 10
Ilona Stüberl 29
Kardos 57

INDIAN
Koh-i-Noor 40

INTERNATIONAL
Altwienerhof 66
Anna Sacher 66
Do & Co 76
Donauturm 76
East to West 59
Hansen 26
Himmelpforte 60
Imperial 67
Kervansaray 60
König von Ungarn 67
Königsbacher bei der
    Oper 20
Lebenbauer 30
Prinz Eugen 61
Vier Jahreszeiten 67
Zum 'Englischen Reiter'
    47
Zum Leupold 31

ITALIAN
Bacaro Rosso 59
Barbaro's 19
Cantinetta Antinori 8
Capriccio da Conte 38
Cavaliere 49
Da Capo 9
Danieli 19
Firenze 26
Francesco 80
Garibaldi Ristorante 60
Grotta Azzurra 29
Martinelli 30
Novelli 26
Oliva Verde 70
Osteria Collavini 20
La Piazza 21
Regina Margherita 30

San Carlo 20
A Tavola 77
La Tavolozza 71
Venezia 21

JAPANESE
Akakiko 36
Akashi 37
Busan Sushi 37
Fuji 37
Fujiyama 10
Kiang Noodles 37
Tenmaya 37
Toko-Ri 37
Tokyo 37
Unkai 37
Yohm 11, 37

MEDITERRANEAN
Aioli 8
Dalmatia 9

MEXICAN
Pepito 61

MONGOLIAN
Mongolian Barbecue 40

NORTHWEST
AFRICAN
Al Badaui 29

SOUTH AMERICAN
Lima 70
Maredo 50

STYRIAN
Steirereck 57

TURKISH
Kervansaray 60
Lale 40
Levante 30, 70

VEGETARIAN
Siddhartha 51, 89
Wrenkh 41, 89

VIENNESE
Alt-Sievering 86
Alter Klosterkeller im
    Passauer-hof 78
Altes Bürgermeisterhaus
    76
Altes Jägerhaus 46
Altes Presshaus 78
Anna Sacher 66
Augustiner-Keller 19
Bach-Hengl 78
Bamkraxler 76
Boheme 69

Braunsperger 87
Brummbärli 80
Café Imperial 26
Le Ciel 66
Cobenzl 76
Drei Husaren 10
Eckel 87
Engelhardt Restaurant
    'Zur schönen
    Aussicht' 80
Esterházykeller 29
Fadringer 38
Familie Muth 80
Feuerwehr-Wagner 80
Figlmüller 49
Figlmüller's 80
Die fromme Helene 69
Griechenbeisl 50
Grinzingerhof 81
Grünauer 77
Gustl Bauer 40
Hans Maly 81
Hauermandel 81
Hengl-Haselbrunner 82
Heurigenschank 82
Himmelpforte 60
Hotel im Palais
    Schwarzenberg 67
Karl Berger 87
Karrer 69
Kern 30
Kierlinger 87
Kirchenstöckl 82
Kochwerkstatt 70
Königsbacher bei der
    Oper 20
Kornhäuslturm 50
Korso 26
Liane Neumüller 47
Mandahus 87
Mayer am Pfarrplatz 82
Neues Rathaus
    (Hermann Adam) 70
Ofenloch 40
Puklpreiner 61
Rosa Elefant 41
Rudolfshof 83
Schnattl 71
Schöll 77
Schübel-Auer 87
Spatzennest 71
Stadtbeisl 31
Steinschaden 87
Steirereck 57
Weibels Wirtshaus 11
Weingut Reinprecht 83
Weinschlössl 83
Zum Kuckuck 21
Zum Leupold 31
Zum Wilden Mann 47
Zum Zillner 27

Stephansdom

The streets around Vienna's most illustrious landmark are full of lively cafés and restaurants. Many of them have pavement terraces – ideal for people-watching.

STEPHANSDOM
Restaurants

Aioli ❶

Haas Haus, 3 Stock, Stephanspl. 12

☏ 532 0373

Ⓤ U-Bahn Stephansplatz

Open: daily 1000–0100

Reservations essential

VISA

Mediterranean

€€–€€€

Ensconced on the third floor of the Haas Haus (with views of the Stephansdom), Aioli's virtues include a welcome absence of culinary pretence. The pasta dishes are a delight, the homemade garlic mayonnaise a revelation. Start with Spanish *tapas* or a selection from the *antipasti* buffet. The fish is flown in daily from Barcelona. Small terrace.

Cantinetta Antinori ❷

Jasomir-Gottstr. 3–5

☏ 533 7722

Ⓤ U-Bahn Stephansplatz

Open: daily 1130–1430, 1800–2400

Reservations recommended

All credit cards accepted

Italian

€€€

Any Italian will tell you that the fundamental ingredient of a perfect meal is extra-virgin olive oil. Here it comes straight from the Antinori estates outside Florence, as do the wonderful Chianti Classico wines. Tuscan specialities to look out for include *pappa al pomodoro* and veal in cream of truffle sauce, but give the swordfish due consideration.

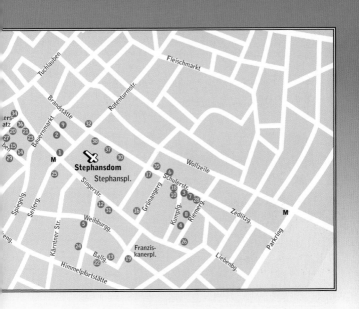

Da Capo

Schulerstr. 18

☎ 512 4491

Ⓤ U-Bahn Stephansplatz

Open: daily 1130–0030

Reservations recommended

▭▭▭

Italian

€€–€€€

A cross between a pizzeria and a *ristorante*, Da Capo welcomes its customers with good, no-frills Italian food at very reasonable prices. There are seasonal as well as à la carte menus featuring more than 20 pizza toppings, pastas, risottos, fish and seafood dishes. Recommendation: tomato soup with basil followed by baked trout with rosemary. If you want to eat on the terrace, you'll need to book.

Dalmatia

Riemerg. 12

☎ 513 2992

Ⓤ U-Bahn Stubentor

Open: Mon–Sat 1130–1430, 1730–2300

Reservations recommended

▭▭ ⓓ American Express

Mediterranean

€€

Large, modern fish restaurant, somewhat lacking in atmosphere but appealing if you're into the cuisine of the former Yugoslavia. Sea devil, sea bream, salmon and scampi are all on the menu or you could try the seafood or mixed fish platters. Also pastas, risottos and

▲ Haas Haus

some meat dishes. Croatian and Italian wines.

Drei Husaren

Weihburgg. 4

✆ 512 1092

🅟 U-Bahn Stephansplatz

Open: daily 1200–1500, 1800–0100

Reservations recommended

All credit cards accepted

Viennese

💶💶💶

If the Habsburgs were ever to return to Vienna, this is the kind of place they'd probably feel at home in. Over the years, the 'Three Hussars' has established an enviable reputation for impeccable service and classy Viennese cooking (the hors-d'oeuvres trolley is the stuff of legend). If the bill comes as a bit of a shock, put it down to the wine.

Fujiyama

Schulerstr. 13

✆ 512 8669

🅟 U-Bahn Stephansplatz

Open: daily 1100–2300

Reservations recommended

All credit cards accepted

Japanese

💶💶–💶💶💶

The speciality here is *yakitori* (assorted pieces of grilled chicken – breast, wings, gizzard, liver, heart) served on skewers. If this doesn't appeal, go for the sushi and *tempura* dishes or opt instead for the daily set menu (available Mon–Fri 1100–1700).

Gulaschmuseum

Schulerstr. 20

✆ 512 1017

🅟 U-Bahn Stephansplatz or Stubentor

Open: Mon–Fri 0900–2400, Sat–Sun 1000–2400

Reservations essential

💳 💶

Hungarian

💶💶

An excellent value lunch stop, Gulaschmuseum currently offers 15 different varieties of the Hungarian favourite, including fish and mushoom. The menu is available in five languages and with pictures to boot, so there's little chance of ordering the wrong meal! Brisk but friendly service and a fast turnover.

Saint Michel

Riemerg. 14

✆ 512 5701

🅟 U-Bahn Stubentor

Open: Mon–Sat 1100–2400

Reservations recommended

All credit cards accepted

French

💶💶

This informal French bistro brings the

flavours of the Parisian Left Bank to the heart of Vienna. Daily specials might include *soupe à l'oignon des Halles*, *confit de canard* or oysters while the à la carte menu ranges from *filet de rascasse* (scorpion fish) to *cotelette d'agneau* (lamb cutlet). Salads, crêpes and *croques monsieurs* also available.

Shanghai 9

Jasomir-gottstr. 6

✆ 533 7419

Ⓤ U-Bahn Stephansplatz

Open: daily 1200–1500, 1800–2330

Reservations unnecessary

All credit cards accepted

Chinese

€€

Pagodas and Chinese lanterns may be the ultimate cliché but there's more to this restaurant than meets the eye. Shanghai cuisine is sweeter and oilier than Cantonese and makes great play with soy sauce. The classic dish is *xiao long bao* – a round steamed dumpling with a wheaten wrapper and juicy pork filling. As well as 14 types of soup, the menu here includes tofu and fish specialities as well as the usual beef and duck.

Weibels Wirtshaus 10

Kumpfg. 2

✆ 512 3986

Ⓤ Stephansplatz

Open: Mon–Sat 1130–2400

Reservations recommended

💳 💳

Viennese

€€€

Gourmand Hans Weibel was pulling everyone's leg when he called this superior restaurant a *Wirtshaus* (tavern or inn). He certainly knows a thing or two about wines, one reason why discerning Austrians continue to flock here. The other attraction is the simple but elegant Viennese cooking. Garden terrace.

Yohm 11

Peterspl. 3

✆ 533 2900

Ⓤ U-Bahn Stephansplatz

Open: daily 1120–1500, 1800–2400

Reservations unnecessary

All credit cards accepted

Asian

€€

The latest addition to Vienna's growing list of sushi bars, Yohm occupies a prime site on the lovely square behind the Stephansdom. In fact, the menu is Asian fusion rather than pure Japanese, with tandoori chicken and Siam beef salad featuring along-side the likes of *miso* soup and *udon* noodles with vegetables and basil. The hot lime tart makes an interesting dessert.

▲ Goulash, Gulaschmuseum

STEPHANSDOM
Bars, cafés and pubs

Akakiko 12

Singerstr. 4

✆ 513 7946

Ⓜ U-Bahn Stephansplatz

Open: daily 1030–2400

€

The most central of the three Akakiko sushi bars. Exotic fast food off the conveyor belt. Menu in German and Japanese only.

Ball Café 13

Ballg. 5

✆ 513 1754

Ⓜ U-Bahn Stephansplatz

Open: Mon–Sat 1030–0200, Sun 1200–2400

€–€€

Hidden away in a tiny side street, the dark vaulted interior of this lovely café with wooden furnishings and marble-top tables is the perfect ambience for working off stress. Irish coffee is a speciality here or there's a choice of Earl Grey and flavoured teas. The menu caters for most tastes with a choice of Middle Eastern dishes as well as lasagne, Schnitzels, ham and eggs and grilled trout – or you could make do with a filled baguette or strudel.

Café Europe 14

Graben 31

✆ 533 1052

Ⓜ U-Bahn Stephansplatz

Open: daily 0700–2400

€

An espresso bar straight out of the 1950s, Café de l'Europe, to give it its formal name, has a first-floor location overlooking the Graben. The speciality here is not coffees but wines and spirits, so you might enjoy a schnaps with your shrimp cocktail or ham roll.

Chattanooga 15

Graben 29a

✆ 533 5000

Ⓜ U-Bahn Stephansplatz

Open: daily 0700–0200

€–€€

The big plus here is the terrace on the Graben. The menu (in English with pictures) is typically fast food – spare ribs, chilli con carne, chicken in the basket, all with chips.

La Crêperie 16

Grünangerg. 10

✆ 512 5687

Ⓜ U-Bahn Stephansplatz

Open: Mon–Fri 1600–2400, Sat–Sun 1100–2400

€€

The name says it all – well, not quite. You might also be tempted by the *escargots*, *soupe à l'oignon, bouillebaisse* and *saumon fumée royale*. There's even a gourmet menu, as well as special dishes for children.

Dom-Beisl 17

Schulerstr. 4

✆ 512 9181

Ⓜ U-Bahn Stephansplatz

Open: Mon–Thu 1100–1930, Fri 1100–1500

€–€€

The main attractions of this crowded, rather impersonal *Beisl* are the daily specials and Gold Fassl beer on draught. Not for anyone averse to cigarette smoke.

First American Bar 18

Kumpfg.1/Schulerstr. 16

✆ 513 2207

Ⓜ U-Bahn Stephansplatz

Open: daily 1600–0100

€

BALL Café/Restaurant

A cocktail bar first and foremost, First American also sells malt whiskies, Irish coffee and hot punch. Happy hour Mon–Sat 1700–2000.

Kleines Café ⓲

Franziskanerpl. 3

∅ None available

Ⓤ U-Bahn Stephansplatz

Open: Mon–Sat 1000–0200, Sun 1300–0200

€

Cosy and friendly, this popular café has a great location on the square. It's always a tight squeeze in the two small rooms, so eating lunch here is usually an elbow-to-elbow affair. Menu highlights include peasant omelette and a good selection of open sandwiches. Speciality drink: *Zehner-Mischung* (rum, orange juice and red wine).

Panino ⓴

Trattnerhof 2

∅ 533 9907

Ⓤ U-Bahn Stephansplatz

Open: Mon–Sat 1100–2400

€

Unpretentious Italian eatery with a takeaway counter downstairs and café on the first floor. Light menu of mainly salads, filled rolls and desserts.

Sparky's Bar and Grill ㉑

Goldschmiedg. 8

∅ 533 6155

Ⓤ U-Bahn Stephansplatz

Open: daily 1000–0200

€€

▲ Stephansdom, Stephansplatz

American cocktail bar, also specialising in Creole cooking.

Zum Alten Blumenstock ㉒

Ballg. 6

∅ 513 1704

Ⓤ U-Bahn Stephansplatz

Open: daily 1100–0200

€€

The building dates back to the 17th century, the food is traditional Viennese (goulash, turkey fillet, and so on), while the clientele are predominantly young. Lively atmosphere.

Zum Weisshappel ㉓

Goldschmiedg. 9

∅ 533 9096

Ⓤ U-Bahn Stephansplatz

Open: Mon–Fri 1000–1500, 1800–2100, Sat 1000–1500

€€

This famous delicatessen near the Peterskirche sells only the freshest home-grown produce. Upstairs is a café-restaurant serving meaty Viennese *Hausmannskost*: beef soup with garlic dumplings, pig's heart, lamb cutlets, *Tafelspitz* with roast potatoes and apple sauce.

STEPHANSDOM
Shops, markets and picnic sites

Bakers and confectioners

Bäckerei Wenninger 24

Rauchensteing. 4

🚇 U-Bahn Stephansplatz

Open: Mon–Fri 0600–1800, Sat 0730–1630

Small 'to go' bakery selling cakes and pastries as well as novelty breads and soft drinks.

Confisserie 25

Seilerg. 2

🚇 U-Bahn Stephansplatz

Open: Mon–Fri 1000–1800, Sat 1100–1600

A small confectioner's full to bursting with sweets and chocolates, also cakes and pastries 26.

Fabienne 26

Riemerg. 1–3

🚇 U-Bahn Stephansplatz

Open: Mon–Fri 0900–1830, Sat 0900–1330

Every chocolate-lover's dream, Fabienne's ranges include Belgian specialities.

Gelateria Italiana 27

Trattenhof 3

🚇 U-Bahn Stephansplatz

Open: daily 1100–2300; closed Nov–Feb

This ice-cream parlour sells its own brand.

Plenty of flavours to choose from.

Johann Wolfbauer 28

Schulerstr. 22

🚇 U-Bahn Stubentor

Open: Mon–Fri 0600–1430

This famous baker's and confectioner's was founded in the days of the Habsburgs. Apart from fresh bread, there's a tempting range of filled sandwiches (spinach and ricotta, tomato and mozzarella, ham and zucchini, salami and broccoli, for example).

Lehmann 29

Graben 12

🚇 U-Bahn Stephansplatz

Open: Mon–Sat 0800–1900

This *Café-Konditorei* has a prime site in the heart of Imperial Vienna. Breakfast is served from 0800, while later in the day you can enjoy the traditional coffee and cake, either on the premises or with a picnic.

United Chocolates 30

Stephanspl. 11

🚇 U-Bahn Stephansplatz

Open: Mon–Sat 0800–1900

This confectioner's is right outside the Stephansdom.

Grocers and supermarkets

Bila 31

Singerstr. 8

🚇 U-Bahn Stephansplatz

Open: Mon–Wed 0800–1900, Thu–Fri 0730–1900, Sat 0730–1800

Branch of the well-known Austrian supermarket chain.

Duran 32

Rotenturmstr. 11

🚇 U-Bahn Stephansplatz

Open: Mon–Fri 0730–1900

Sandwich bar with a deli counter at the front of the shop and tables at the back if you want to sit down for a snack. Menu includes liver dumpling soup, goulash, Serbian kebabs (*čevapčiči*) and Schnitzel with potato salad.

Julius Meinl 33

Am Graben

🚇 U-Bahn Stephansplatz

Open: Mon–Sat 0800–1900

The main branch of the famous Austrian supermarket chain. Gift-wrapped foods of all kinds, regional specialities, international cheeses and cafeteria (first floor).

Waldland 34

Peterspl. 11

U-Bahn Stephansplatz
Open: Mon–Fri 0900–1800, Sat 0900–1700, Sun 0900–1300

Specialist shop, showcasing produce from Austria's Waldviertel region. Most prominent are foodstuffs made with poppy seeds, including cakes and breads – there's even a poppy-seed liqueur! Also marmalades, Kirsch, spices, cheeses and Waldviertel whisky.

Weiser 35

Schulerstr. 3

U-Bahn Stephansplatz
Open: Mon–Fri 0700–1800

This old-fashioned butcher's was founded in 1875. Apart from sausages and hams, there's a large delicatessen counter and *rôtisserie*.

Wienerwald 36

Goldschmiedg. 6

U-Bahn Stephansplatz
Open: daily 0800–2000

This is the takeaway counter of the cafeteria. Sells soups, sandwiches, salads, cheeseburgers and other snacks.

Wines

Heiligenkreuzer Gwölb 37

Stephanspl. 7

U-Bahn Stephansplatz
Open: Mon–Fri 0900–1900, Sat 0900–1700

This wine merchant's, on the Rotenturm corner of Stephansplatz, sells presentation-packaged drinks, including spirits and liqueurs; also honey, jams and preserves.

Vinothek St Stephan 38

Stephanspl. 6

U-Bahn Stephansplatz
Open: Mon–Fri 0900–1830, Sat 0930–1300

This emporium claims to be Vienna's leading wine merchant. It showcases each of Austria's wine producing regions and is also a major importer.

▲ Lehmann

The Viennese coffeehouse

Places of legend

The coffeehouse, one of the great Viennese institutions, is all things to all men (and women) – a place to think, write, relax, read the newspapers, play cards, do business, set the world to rights, or conduct a dangerous (or perfectly innocent) liaison. Essentially coffeehouses are for whiling away the time. You only need to buy one drink and no one will disturb you, let alone ask you to leave. The Austrian writer Peter Altenberg even gave the Café Central as his postal address!

The first coffeehouse opened shortly after the Turkish siege of Vienna in 1683 and the idea quickly took off. Over time customers became increasingly fussy about how they wanted their coffee served – in a cup or glass, black or with a dollop of cream, with rum, orange, brandy, egg yolk …

Each coffeehouse attracts its own fiercely loyal clientele. Actors and journalists frequent Landtmann, intellectuals gather in Bräunerhof, artists favour Hawelka, Bellaria attracts politicians, bankers congregate at Café Central, Frauenhuber is for civil servants, students and academics hang out at Haag, while Sacher and Demel are usually full of tourists! In the more formal establishments it's customary to order your coffee from the waiting staff before inspecting the counter displays of strudels, *Buchteln* (jam buns) and *Torten* (cakes). Many cafés also serve hot dishes and set lunches.

- **Café Central** *Herreng. 14; ✆ 533 3763-0; Ⓜ U-Bahn Karlsplatz; open: Mon–Sat 0800–2000, Sun 1000–1800; ●.* Though not what it was, the Central's vaulted halls still have an air of opulence – it's hard to believe that Leon Trotsky was one of the regulars. The speciality of the house is the *Pharisäer* (black coffee with rum, sugar and whipped cream) and there are also snacks and simple hot and cold dishes including desserts.
- **Café Griensteidl** (*see page 32*)
- **Café Sacher** *Philharmonikerstr. 4; ✆ 514 56-0; Ⓜ U-Bahn Karlsplatz; open: daily 1130–1500, 1800–2330; ●●.* Famous for the dessert invented by Franz Sacher, the pastry chef of Austria's foreign minister, Prince Metternich, in 1832. The décor – red wallpaper, carpets, brocaded chairs, lustres, the obligatory portraits of Franz Joseph and Sissi and tall mirrors made to look like windows – is all rather claustrophobic and there are so many tourists that it's difficult to find a table at the height of the season. If all you've come for is

the Sachertorte, you'd do just as well buying it from the shop round the corner (*Kärntnerstr. 38; open: Mon-Sat 0900-1800*) and eating it at home!

• **Demel** *Kohlmarkt 14; ℗ 535 1717-0;* 🚇 *U-Bahn Herrengasse; open: daily 0930-1930;* ❸. The stunning rococo interior of the former court baker's takes one's breath away. When you've recovered, look through the menu and you'll find a choice of sixty pastries alone. And then there are the coffees …!

• **Diglas** (*see page 53*)

• **Frauenhuber** *Himmelpfortg. 6; ℗ 512 4323;* 🚇 *U-Bahn Stephansplatz; open: Mon-Fri 0800-2300, Sat 0800-1600;* ❸❸. Vienna's oldest surviving coffeehouse first opened its doors in 1824. Some years earlier, the upstairs room was used for concerts – Mozart and Beethoven both performed here.

• **Hawelka** *Dorotherg. 6; ℗ 512 8230;* 🚇 *U-Bahn Herrengasse; open: Mon-Sat 0800-0200, Sun 1600-0200;* ❸. Popular with artistic types of every description, the atmospere in this *Lokal* is always relaxed and convivial. There's not much in the way of food, apart from the wonderful *Buchteln* (doughnuts with vanilla sauce).

• **Landtmann** *Dr Karl-Lueger-Ring 4; ℗ 532 0621;* 🚇 *U-Bahn Schottentor; open: daily 0800-2400;* ❸-❸❸. Sigmund Freud was the most famous patron of this busy café, located on a hectic corner opposite the

▲ Café Sacher

Rathaus. In the summer the worldly wise clientele spills out on to the large covered terrace, while those left indoors pore over the newspapers. The lunch dishes include traditional Viennese favourites such as Schnitzel and *Tafelspitz*, and the homemade desserts are also good.

… a place to think, write, relax, read the newspapers, play cards, do business and set the world to rights …

• **Votiv** *Reichsratstr. 17; ℗ 406 5913;* 🚇 *U-Bahn Schottentor; open: Mon-Fri 0800-2000, Sat-Sun 1000-1800;* ❸❸. This roomy, but very smoky *Lokal* is popular with students. The green-and-rose décor dates from a renovation in 1990 and is now rather faded. Specialities of the day such as grilled scampi and ham omelette on ciabatta, are written up on a blackboard, while the à la carte includes toast, pasta dishes and fresh desserts. You can order a pot of fruit tea if you're not in the mood for coffee.

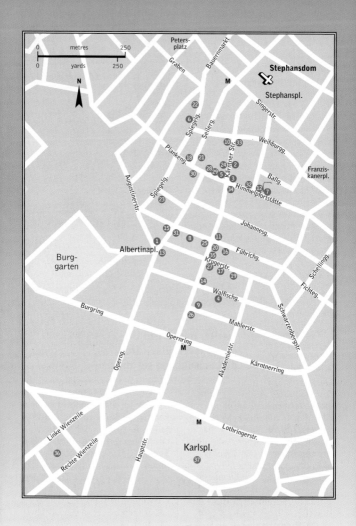

Petersplatz

Graben

Bauernmarkt

M

✠ Stephansdom

Stephanspl.

Singerstr.

Weihburgg.

Spiegelg.

Seilerg.

22

6

Plankeng.

Kärntner Str.

10 33

18

21

24 29

2

Augustinerstr.

Spiegelg.

28 29

5

30

3

32 12 7

34

Himmelpfortstätte

Franziskanerpl.

Ballg.

Johannesg.

15 31

8

11

1

Albertinapl.

13

25

20

16

35

Führichg.

Krugerstr.

27

17

14

19

Burg-
garten

Walfischg.

4

9

Burgring

26

Mahlerstr.

Opernring

Operng.

M

Akademiestr.

Kärntnerring

Schwarzenbergstr.

Schellingg.

Fichteg.

Linke Wienzeile

Hauptstr.

M

Lothringerstr.

36

Rechte Wienzeile

Karlspl.

37

N

0   metres   250
0   yards   250

Kärntnerstrasse

Vienna's main shopping street hosts numerous fast-food outlets as well as more formal restaurants.

KÄRNTNERSTRASSE
Restaurants

Augustiner-Keller

Augustinerstr. 1

✆ 533 1026

Ⓜ U-Bahn Karlsplatz

Open: daily 1100–2400 (Sat until 0100)

Reservations unnecessary

All credit cards accepted

Viennese

€€

This well-known wine cellar near the Staatsoper (State Opera House) belongs firmly in the folksy Viennese *Heurige* tradition. There's the usual hot and cold buffet selection with wine from the monastic estates and an all-inclusive offer if you come here in the evening. Live *Schrammelmusik* performances begin at 1830.

Barbaro's

Kärntnerstr. 19

✆ 513 1712

Ⓜ U-Bahn Stephansplatz

Open: daily 1200–1500, 1800–0100

Reservations recommended

All credit cards accepted

Italian-Fusion

€€€

This Italian restaurant, with views across the rooftops of Vienna, is currently fashionable with the city's wheelers and dealers. The fusion food, an unusual combination of Italian and Asian influences, is appealing but over-priced. Book ahead, especially if you want a table on the terrace (summer only).

Danieli

Himmelpfortg. 3

✆ 513 7913

Ⓜ U-Bahn Stephansplatz

Open: daily 1000–0200

Reservations unnecessary

💳 ⓐ American Express

Italian

€€

Pizzas are what they do best in this busy but friendly *osteria* where the kitchen stays open into the small hours. Otherwise, it's the usual mixture of risotto, pasta, meat and fish dishes.

▲ Kärntnerstrasse

▲ Orpheus

Königsbacher bei der Oper ④

Walfischg. 5

☎ 513 1210

Ⓤ U-Bahn Karlsplatz

Open: Mon–Fri 1000–2400,
Sat 1000–1600

Reservations essential

▨ American Express

Viennese-International

❸❸

The tag means 'by the
opera house'. This popu-
lar Viennese brasserie
fills up quickly, espe-
cially in the evening on
account of the prices.
The Austrian cuisine is
fairly predictable but
the salads are good and
taste even better on the
terrace in summer.

Lucky Chinese ⑤

Kärntnerstr. 24

☎ 512 3428

Ⓤ U-Bahn Stephansplatz

Open: daily 1130–2400

Reservations unnecessary

All credit cards accepted

Chinese

❸❸

High-street Chinese on
the first floor, above

Club 24. The cooking is
flavoured with fiery
sauces typical of dishes
from the province of
Szechuan. Also
Taiwanese specialities.

Orpheus ⑥

Spiegelg. 10

☎ 512 3888

Ⓤ U-Bahn Stephansplatz

Open: Sun–Thu 1200–2400,
Fri–Sat 1200–0100

Reservations recommended

All credit cards accepted

Greek

❸❸

While the formal dining
room is more Viennese
than Hellenic, the cui-
sine is the real McCoy
and includes Cretan
specialities. The home-
produced olive oil adds
flavour to the lamb
grills and kebabs and
the fish too is appetis-
ing. Usual range of
mezédes (starters) with
sickly sweet *baklava* for
dessert.

Osteria Collavini ⑦

Himmelpfortg. 17

☎ 512 6699

Ⓤ U-Bahn Stephansplatz

Open: Mon 1800–2330,
Tue–Sat 1130–1430, 1800–
2330

Reservations recommended

All credit cards accepted

Italian

❸❸

Cheap and cheerful
Italian trattoria in the
heart of the shopping
district. No-frills
cooking, but excellent
homemade pasta and,
for once, reasonably
priced wine.

La Piazza ⑧

Führichg. 1

☎ 512 6233

Ⓤ U-Bahn Stephansplatz

Open: daily 1000–2400

Reservations unnecessary

All credit cards accepted

Italian-Austrian

❸❸

Near the Albertina end
of the Hofburg, La
Piazza could make a
convenient lunch stop.
The pizzas, cooked in a
wood-fired oven, are
just as they should be,
but there's also plenty of
choice from among the
pasta, fish and meat
dishes. Excellent salad
buffet. No-smoking area.

San Carlo ⑨

Mahlerstr. 3

☎ 513 8984

Ⓤ U-Bahn Karlsplatz

Open: Mon–Sat 1200–1430,
1830–2400

Reservations recommended

▨

Italian

❸❸❸

This Italian restaurant is in the shopping arcade known as the Ringstrassegalerien. Rather old-fashioned in appearance, it's proud to advertise 'no pizzas'. What they do offer are tried and tested favourites such as *saltimbocca alla Romana* (rolled veal and ham), *coda di rospo* (monkfish), *scampi alla marinara* and *soglila al vino bianco* (sole in white wine). The wine list is eminently respectable and includes Barolo, Villa Antinori and Verdicchio.

Venezia

Kärntnerstr. 10

✆ 512 6234

🚇 U-Bahn Stephansplatz

Open: daily 1100–2300

Reservations recommended

💳 ⓓ American Express

Italian

💰💰

This Italian eatery near Stephansplatz covers two floors. At ground level there's a pizzeria and takeaway counter, while the restaurant upstairs serves the usual mixture of pasta, meat and seafood dishes. Children's portions available. Pavement tables on Kärntnerstrasse.

Wienerwald

Annag. 3

✆ 512 3766

🚇 U-Bahn Stephansplatz

Open: daily 1100–2400

Reservations recommended

All credit cards accepted

Austrian

💰💰

One of a chain of Viennese restaurants that seems to find favour with 'women who lunch'– maybe it's the raspberry dumplings that appeal. Otherwise, the menu includes *Backhändel* (fried chicken), goulash, Schnitzels, burgers and salads.

Zum Kuckuck

Himmelpfortg. 15

✆ 512 8470

🚇 U-Bahn Stephansplatz

Open: Mon–Sat 1200–1430, 1800–2400

Reservations recommended

All credit cards accepted

Viennese

💰💰–💰💰💰

This well-regarded restaurant appeals to traditionalists, though the cooking (game and fish) makes at least a nod in the direction of nouvelle cuisine. Well suited to a romantic dinner. Special gourmet menu.

▲ Venezia

KÄRNTNERSTRASSE
Bars, cafés and pubs

Café Mozart 🔞

Albertinapl. 2

☏ 513 0801

🚇 U-Bahn Karlsplatz

Open: daily 0800–2400

€–€€

Although this café is more than 200 years old, there's no actual connection with the composer. The typically elegant décor has been beautifully restored and there are charming views of historic Albertinaplatz. Espionage is the last thing you'd associate it with, yet interestingly the founding head of Austria's secret police, Count Metternick, was a regular here in the 1840s and the café later featured in the classic spy thriller, *The Third Man*. Newspapers include the *Herald Tribune* and the menu features English breakfast with Earl Grey, warm dishes and a choice of classic coffees. Takes all credit cards.

Café Sirk 🔞

Kärntnerstr. 53

☏ 515 16509

🚇 U-Bahn Karlsplatz

Open: daily 1000–2400

€€

Across the road from the Staatsoper, Café Sirk is more like a bar than a traditional coffeehouse. On the menu is *Paradeissuppe* (tomato soup), opera platter (roast beef with shrimps), salmon pie and rice soufflé with raspberry sauce.

Café Tirolerhof 🔞

Tegetthoffstr. 8

☏ 512 7833

🚇 U-Bahn Stephansplatz

Open: Mon–Sat 0700–2100, Sun 0930–2000

€–€€

This superbly restored Biedermeier café has remained true to its bourgeois origins. While the food is not particularly appetising, you can pick up a sandwich or light snack here. A useful stop on the way to the Kaisergruft (Imperial mausoleum).

Cherie 🔞

Annag. 12

▲ Gerstner

512 4789

U-Bahn Stephansplatz

Open: daily 1000–0100

€

This cocktail bar, off Kärntnerstrasse, also serves Warsteiner beer on draught, single-dish lunches (Wiener Schnitzel, goulash) and ice creams.

Coffeeshop Company

Krugerstr. 6

512 0844

U-Bahn Stephansplatz

Open: Mon–Sat 0700–2300, Sun 1000–2200

€–€€

West-coast-style American coffee shop with coffee 'to go' or drink in. Also a mouth-watering array of freshly baked bagels, muffins, brownies, cookies, croissants and doughnuts.

Konditorei Oberlaa Stadthaus ⑱

Neuer Markt 16

512 2936

U-Bahn Karlsplatz, Stephansplatz

Open: Mon–Fri 0800–1900, Sat 0800–1800, Sun 1000–1800

€€

Smart, rather formal *pâtisserie*, specialising in high-quality cakes and pastries. Also Oberlaa breakfast and appealing two-course lunches served from 1100 until 1500. Try cream of carrot soup, baby mozzarella and salad or roast dumpling with egg.

Krugerhof ⑲

Krugerstr. 8

512 5285

U-Bahn Stephansplatz

Open: Mon–Fri 0700–2200, Sat 0700–1600

€–€€

Popular with students and young people, this well-known café has two billiard tables at the back. The meals are plain but cheap – ham and eggs, stuffed peppers, Wiener Schnitzel and *Eierschwammerl* (egg and mushroom).

New York, New York ⑳

Annag. 8

513 8651

U-Bahn Stephansplatz

Open: Mon–Thu 1700–0200, Fri 1700–0300, Sat 1900–0300

€

The star of this American-style cocktail bar off Kärntnerstrasse is virtuoso mixer, Farhat Ellouzi (former bartender of the year). Happy hour 1700 until 1900.

Priemer ㉑

Neuer Markt 2

512 9202

U-Bahn Stephansplatz

Open: daily 1100–0100

€€

Homely café-restaurant specialising in German cuisine. Incidentally, it was in the next-door house that the composer Josef Haydn wrote the

Kaiserlied, better known now as the German national anthem.

Pronto ㉒

Spiegelg. 2

513 1900

U-Bahn Stephansplatz

Open: Mon–Sat 1100–0200

€€

The cooking in this stylish café-bar, near Stock-im-Eisen Platz, is Italian with Venetian specialities. No pizzas.

Reinthaler ㉓

Gluckg. 5

512 3366

U-Bahn Stephansplatz

Open: Mon–Sat 0900–2300 (Fri until 2200)

€€

An attractive *Beisl* in the heart of the city, Reinthaler offers very acceptable *Hausmannskost* (home cooking) as well as simple breakfasts. Typical dishes include gypsy cutlet and roast liver.

Reiss ㉔

Marco d'Aviano G. 1

512 7198

U-Bahn Stephansplatz

▲ Wild

Open: Mon–Fri 1100–0300,
Sat 1000–0300, Sun 1100–
0300

€€

Small, ultra-modern
oyster and champagne
bar with pine wood
décor and white marble
tables. Other luxuries
include caviar.

Rosenberger Marktrestaurant ㉕

Maysederg. 2/Fürichg. 3

✆ 512 3458

Ⓜ U-Bahn Karlsplatz

Open: daily 1030–2300

€–€€

This enormous self-
service cafeteria occu-
pies the lower-ground
floor of the Rosenberger
food store (*see page
25*). The dining space is
divided into themed
corners – coffeehouse,
Heurige, grandma's
kitchen, and so on.
Large no-smoking area.
Takes all credit cards.

Segafredo ㉖

Mahlerstr. 4

✆ 512 7330

Ⓜ U-Bahn Stephansplatz

Open: Mon–Thu 0800–2330,
Fri–Sat 0800–2400, Sun
1100–2100

€

Handy for shopping,
this Italian café is in the
mall known as the
Ringstrassegalerien. The
snacks are appetising
and include *tramezzini*
(Italian sandwiches),
focaccia (a kind of
pizza) and filled rolls.
Breakfasts also avail-
able. Happy hour 2000
until 2200.

Siam ㉗

Krugerstr. 6

✆ 533 5235

Ⓜ U-Bahn Stephansplatz

Open: daily 1130–1430,
1730–2400

€€

Café serving sushi and
other Asian dishes.
Fixed price 'all you can
eat' buffet lunch avail-
able from 1130.
Children's portions.

TGI Fridays ㉘

Neuer Markt 8

✆ 513 7789

Ⓜ U-Bahn Stephansplatz

Open: Sun–Thu 1130–0100,
Fri–Sat 1130–0200

€€

Convenient if you've
just been visiting the
Kaisersgruft (Imperial
mausoleum), this large
branch of the well-
known chain has a
typically wide-ranging
menu, from barbecued
ribs and *filet mignon* to
Caesar salad, *fajitas*,
quesadillas and mocha
mud pie.

Trattoria al Caminetto ㉙

Neuer Markt 8a

✆ 512 3442

Ⓜ U-Bahn Stephansplatz

Open: daily 1000–2400

€€

Small Italian restaurant
with a good line in fish
as well as meat dishes –
bistecca alla Fiorentina
(beefsteak), *saltimbocca*
(rolled veal and ham)
and lamb cutlets. The
large terrace facing the
square fills up quickly
at lunchtimes.

Wild ㉚

Neuer Markt 10–11

✆ 512 5303

Ⓜ U-Bahn Stephansplatz

Open: Mon–Fri 0830–1830,
Sat 0830–1300

€

Bakery and delicatessen,
serving hot meals as
well as sandwiches. If
you're planning on a
picnic, there's a fruit
and veg stall outside.

KÄRNTNERSTRASSE
Shops, markets and picnic sites

Bakers and confectioners

Bonbons Anzinger ③①

Tegetthofstr. 5

🚇 U-Bahn Stephansplatz

Open: Mon–Fri 0800–1800, Sat 0800–1300

Sweet shop with an enticing window display of quality chocolates, jellies, marzipan and the ubiquitous *Mozartkugeln*.

Fontanive Emilio ③②

Himmelpfortg. 11

🚇 U-Bahn Stephansplatz

Open: Mon–Sat 1000–2300, Sun 1400–2300

Italian ice-cream parlour, serving 25 different flavours, including the speciality: *Trüffeleis*.

Gerstner ③③

Kärntnerstr. 11–15

🚇 U-Bahn Stephansplatz

Open: Mon–Sat 0900–2000, Sun 1000–2000

Famous pastry shop (founded 1847), formerly purveyors to the Imperial court. Sells gift-wrapped chocolate boxes, sugary confections of various kinds and novelty sweets.

L. Heiner ③④

Kärntnerstrasse 21–3

🚇 U-Bahn Stephansplatz

Open: Mon–Sat 0830–1900, Sun 1000–1900

Imperial confectioner's, turning out marzipans, strudels, truffles and chocolates to order.

Opern Confiserie ③⑤

Kärntnerstr. 47

🚇 U-Bahn Karlsplatz

Open: Mon–Sat 0830–1900, Sun 1000–1900

The chocolate aroma here is almost overpowering. All varieties, including liqueurs, also jellies, macaroons, marrons glacés, *Mozartkugeln*. A place to shop for presents.

Grocers and supermarkets

Rosenberger Marktrestaurant ③⑥

Maysederg. 2/Fürichg. 3

🚇 U-Bahn Karlsplatz

Open: daily 0730–2300

This large food shop specialises in luxury items and gift-wrapped comestibles.

Markets

Naschmarkt ③⑦

🚇 U-Bahn Karlsplatz

Open: Mon–Fri 0600–1830, Sat 0600–1700

Vienna's largest outdoor food market boasts numerous fruit and veg stalls as well as a fine selection of snack bars: **Nordsee** Stands 1–5; **Akakiko** Stand 126; **Indian Pavillon** Stands 74–5; **Heindl & Co** Stands 130–8.

Picnic sites

Karlsplatz ③⑧

🚇 U-Bahn Karlsplatz

An island of serenity in a sea of traffic, Karlsplatz takes its name from the stupendous **Karlskirche**, commissioned by the Emperor Charles VI in 1713, as an act of thanksgiving for deliverance from the plague. One of the pair of delightful pavilions designed by Otto Wagner as underground railway exits in 1898 is now a café and there is seating at various points around the square.

▲ Naschmarkt

Business restaurants

Dining to impress

As Vienna is an international city, playing host to a number of UN organisations, it's well used to catering to the needs of businesses. Most of the leading hotels offer special business lunches and menus.

• **Café Imperial** *Hotel Imperial, Kärntner Ring 16; ✆ 501 10389;* 🔊 *U-Bahn Karlsplatz; open: daily 0700–2300; Viennese;* ❷❷. This elegant, rather formal coffeehouse is perfect for a working breakfast. The buffet is one of the best the city has to offer, though the prices may set your hair on end.

• **Firenze** *Singerstr. 3; ✆ 513 4374;* 🔊 *U-Bahn Stephansplatz; open: daily 1200–1500, 1800–2330; reservations recommended; all credit cards accepted; Italian;* ❷❷–❷❷❷. What appeals most about this Italian restaurant in the Hotel Royal is the terrace on

▲ Firenze

the 10th floor with fabulous views over the rooftops of Vienna. Tuscan and fish specialities include *fegatto di vitello* (veal livers) and *filleti di orata* (sea bream).

• **Hansen** *Wipplingerstr. 34; ✆ 532 0542;* 🔊 *U-Bahn Stephansplatz; open: Mon–Fri 0900–2100, Sat 0900–1700; reservations recommended; all credit cards accepted; International;* ❷❷❷. The basement of the Stock Exchange is now an excellent restaurant with a bright, cheerful ambience and a clientele that knows a good thing when it sees one. The cooking is deft, stylish and good value, while the breakfast grill has its own devotees.

• **Korso** *Hotel Bristol, Mahlerstr. 2; ✆ 515 16546;* 🔊 *U-Bahn Karlsplatz; open: Sun–Fri 1200–1500, Sat 1200–1500; reservations essential; all credit cards accepted; Viennese;* ❷❷❷. Head chef Reinhard Gerer has won numerous accolades for his virtuoso interpretation of classical Viennese cooking. He's ably supported by the sommelier who will guide you through the extensive wine list (the prices leave some diners a little breathless). The three-course business lunch (available Mon–Fri) changes every day and there's a seven-course set menu at dinner.

• **Novelli** *Braünerstr. 11; ✆ 513*

4200; ⓐ *U-Bahn Stephansplatz;*
open: Mon–Sat 1100–0100;
reservations recommended; all
credit cards accepted; Italian;
©©. Standing head and shoulders
above most of its Italian
competitors, Novelli offers great
value for money as well as
quality food. The ambience is
warm and relaxing, the service
attentive but
unobtrusive, the
antipasti
outstanding.

The buffet is one of the best the city has to offer, though the prices may set your hair on end.

• Le Siècle
Radisson SAS
Palais Hotel,
Parkring 16; ℂ
515 170; ⓐ *U-Bahn Stubentor;*
open: daily 1130–1430,
1700–2300; reservations
recommended; all credit cards
accepted; Fish; **©©©**. Located on
the first floor of the hotel, Le
Siècle's main claim to fame is the
wonderful views it offers over the
Stadtpark, though the dining area
itself is lacklustre. The culinary
speciality is fresh seafood and
fish: salmon, sheat, turbot, Creole
red snapper, John Dory and sea
bass are all on the menu but
presentation and quality are not
always of the best, especially
bearing in mind the prices.
There's a set business lunch and a
Sunday brunch with piano
accompaniment.
• Tokyo *Börseg. 3; ℂ 535 0392;*
ⓐ *U-Bahn Schottentor; open:*
Mon–Sat 1130–1430, 1700–
2300; reservations recommended;
all credit cards accepted;
Japanese; **©©©**. This fashionable
Japanese eatery is strong on
ambience but doesn't always
deliver value for money. The
menu is wide-ranging, featuring

the peasant stew known as *shabu
shabu* as well as appetising
selections of sushi and *tempura.*
More unusual are the *sukuyaki*
dishes, where slivers of beef and
vegetables are boiled on a
portable stove, then dipped in
raw egg which warms up and
cooks on the hot food.
• **Walter Bauer** *Sonnenfelsg. 17;*
ℂ 512 9871; ⓐ
U-Bahn
Stephansplatz;
open: Tue–Fri
1200–1400,
1800–2400, Sat
1800–2400;
reservations
essential; ⓓ *American Express;*
Austrian; **©©©**. This classy
establishment is currently rated
among the best in Vienna.
Traditional Austrian dishes are
recreated with unusual subtlety
and lightness of touch, while the
lobster is fast becoming the stuff
of legend. Some may find the
décor a little sugary but this
criticism seems almost churlish
when weighed against the
plusses, which include a wine
cellar worthy of the cuisine and
an excellent choice of schnaps.
• **Zum Zillner** *Dominikanerbastei
22; ℂ 512 7218;* ⓐ *U-Bahn
Schwedenplatz; open: Mon–Fri
1000–2400; reservations
recommended; all credit cards
accepted; Viennese;* **©©**.
Viennese businessmen lunch their
clients at this old-fashioned
hostelry, one of the few genuine
Beisln left in the Altstadt. The
beer (choose from Zipfer,
Goldfassl and Ottakringer) goes
down a treat with the above-
average *Hausmannskost* (home
cooking).

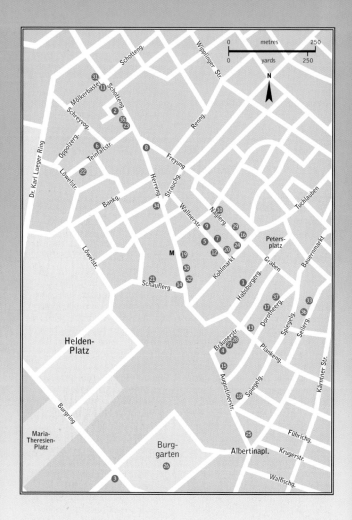

Herrengasse

At the heart of courtly Vienna is Herrengasse, where the Austrian nobility built their palaces. The area has more than its fair share of traditional Viennese cafés and bakeries.

HERRENGASSE
Restaurants

Al Badaui

Habsburgerg. 12a

✆ 533 7925

Ⓤ U-Bahn Herrengasse

Open: Mon–Sat 1800–2400

Reservations recommended

No credit cards accepted

Northwest African

€€

Shades of the North African desert in this elegant Maghreb restaurant. While the cooking isn't especially sophisticated, it's honest and all dishes (*couscous*, *tajine*, and so on) are nicely presented. Suitable for a romantic dinner *à deux*.

Esterhàzykeller

Haarhof 1

✆ 533 3482

Ⓤ U-Bahn Herrengasse

Open: in winter Mon–Fri 1100–2300, Sat–Sun 1600–2300; in summer Mon–Fri 1600–2400

Reservations recommended

All credit cards accepted

Viennese

€€

The wines in this venerable cellar come from the Esterházy estate near the Hungarian border. The food is typical Viennese *Hausmann-skost*, served buffet style, and you can eat either in the brick-vaulted cellar or in one of the equally dark and smoky rooms above.

Grotta Azzurra

Babenbergerstr. 5

✆ 586 1044

Ⓤ U-Bahn Babenbergerstr.

Open: daily 1200–1500, 1830–2400

Reservations recommended

All credit cards accepted

Italian

€€€

Cognoscenti rate this as the best Italian restaurant in the capital and few diners would disagree. The well-lit dining space and stunning blue décor provide the backdrop to an equally brilliant culinary experience. Classic Italian cuisine with wines to match. Recommended: *osso bucco* (knuckle of veal) or any fish dish.

Ilona Stüberl

Bräunerstr. 2

✆ 533 9029

Ⓤ U-Bahn Stephansplatz

▲ Esterhàzykeller buffet

Open: Mon–Sat 1200–1500,
1800–2300

Reservations essential

All credit cards accepted

Hungarian

Authentic Magyar home cooking only a stone's throw from the Graben, and at knock-down prices. While the spicy *Szeginder gulyash* really sets the tastebuds alight, the stuffed peppers and chicken paprika aren't bad either – not to mention the scrumptious filled pancakes for dessert. A shame the surroundings don't inspire the same zest for life.

Kern

Wallnerstr. 3

✆ 533 9188

Ⓤ U-Bahn Herrengasse

Open: Mon–Fri 0800–1800

Reservations recommended

No credit cards accepted

Viennese

Ⓖ Ⓔ

This address was once the private residence of the Emperor Franz Stefan. Now it's a *Beisl* with a certain forced charm. If your stomach's up to it, call in early for the Old Viennese breakfast of goulash, *Würstel* and dumplings, then forget about lunch (and possibly dinner). Other typical dishes include *Beinfleisch*, liver and the ubiquitous Wiener Schnitzel.

Lebenbauer ❻

Teinfaltstr. 3

✆ 533 5556-0

Ⓤ U-Bahn Herrengasse

Open: Mon–Fri 1100–1500,
1800–2300, Sat 1100–
1500

Reservations recommended

All credit cards accepted

International

Ⓖ Ⓔ

An 'in' restaurant that promises quality and usually delivers to a health-conscious clientele. There's an appetising choice of salads and vegetarian dishes to match. Note that the pasta is gluten free (good news for coeliacs!).

Levante ❼

Wallnerstr. 2

✆ 533 2326; takeaway service 523 6301

Ⓤ U-Bahn Herrengasse

Open: daily 1100–2300

Reservations unnecessary

All credit cards accepted

Turkish

Ⓖ Ⓔ

One of a small chain of friendly Turkish restaurants. Start by ordering a selection of *mezes* (starters) – cheese-filled *börek* pastries, *Imam bayildi* (aubergines stuffed with onions, tomatoes and garlic in olive oil), *dolma* (stuffed vegetables) and houmous (creamy paste made with chick peas and flavoured with garlic). You'll be served with pitta bread baked in a wood-fired oven (a real treat) before moving on to the main courses which divide between Levantine pizzas (about 10 choices) and kebabs. If you've a sweet tooth, leave room for the *baklava* (layers of filo pastry and pistachio nuts, coated in syrup) and *halva* (honey cakes).

Martinelli ❽

Freyung 3

✆ 535 3087

Ⓤ U-Bahn Herrengasse

Open: Mon–Sat 1130–1430,
1730–2330

Reservations recommended

All credit cards accepted

Italian

Ⓖ Ⓔ

This sleek, sophisticated trattoria in the wonderfully restored, rococo Palais Harrach specialises in Tuscan cuisine. If you're here during the summer try to book a table on the patio, which looks out on to the 18th-century courtyards known as the Freyung. Excellent wines.

Regina Margherita ❾

Palais Esterházy, Wallnerstr. 4

✆ 533 0812

Ⓤ U-Bahn Herrengasse

Open: daily 1200–1500,
1800–2400 (closed Sun
Oct–Apr)

Reservations recommended

All credit cards accepted

Italian

Ⓖ Ⓔ

The place to head for if you want to sample an authentic quality pizza, cooked using the freshest ingredients by a Neapolitan master baker. Palatial surroundings, good value, pleasant atmosphere and large garden.

Stadtbeisl 🔟

Naglerg. 21

☎ 533 3507

🔴 U-Bahn Herrengasse

Open: daily 1000–2400

Reservations unnecessary

VISA

Viennese

❷❷

A favourite with visitors to Vienna, this restaurant with a vaulted 18th-century interior occupies the site of a medieval monastery and has access to the Viennese catacombs. The standard Austrian fare of Schnitzels, venison goulash, *Beinfleisch* and dumplings is a mite on the heavy side, so loosen your belt, take your time and enjoy the friendly atmosphere.

Zum Leupold 🔟

Schotteng. 7

☎ 533 9381

🔴 U-Bahn Schottentor

Open: daily 1000–2400

Reservations recommended

All credit cards accepted

Viennese-International

❷❷–❷❷❷

This rambling pub-restaurant sets great store by its *Tafelspitz*, apple strudel and other traditional Austrian dishes. Service is on the slow side and the atmosphere a bit impersonal. *Gabelfrühstück* (Viennese brunch) from 1000.

▲ Stadtbeisl

HERRENGASSE
Bars, cafés and pubs

Bistro Anna 12

Wallnerstr. 3

✆ 533 0163

U-Bahn Herrengasse

Open: daily 0800–1100

€€

The menu in this small café off Kohlmarkt includes beefsteak, goulash, Schnitzel, salads and omelettes. Wine by the glass and bottle. Zipfer beer.

Café Bräunerhof 13

Stallburgg. 2

✆ 512 3893

U-Bahn Herrengasse

Open: Mon–Sat 0730–2100, Sun 1000–1900

€€

This classic Viennese coffeehouse, once patronised by writers and opera divas, is ideally suited to anyone who enjoys sitting alone but in company. Patrons can peruse the international press (*Guardian*, *The Times*, *Sunday Express* and *Herald Tribune*) while enjoying a Viennese breakfast, or a Maria Theresia (coffee with orange liqueur and whipped cream). Viennese music at weekends from 1500 until 1800. Lunch menu includes ham omelette, Wiener Schnitzel and *Tafelspitz*.

Café Griensteidl 14

Michaelerpl. 2,

✆ 535 2693-0

U-Bahn Herrengasse

Open: daily 0800–2400

€€

Founded in 1847, Griensteidl is just across the road from the Hofburg. Famous patrons have included the writer Hugo von Hofmannsthal and the composers Hugo Wolff and Arnold Schönberg, while nowadays you're more likely to rub shoulders with journalists from the *Standard* newspaper. Relax in the plush surroundings and choose from the extensive à la carte menu of main courses at lunch, or content yourself with a schnaps or a Fiaker (mocca with Kirsch, served in a glass).

Café Palffy 15

Josefpl. 6

✆ 513 4118

U-Bahn Herrengasse

Open: daily 0900–1900

€

The café enjoys a superb location in a 16th-century palace that was later the venue for a private performance of Mozart's opera, *The Marriage of Figaro*. The menu includes Viennese breakfast and some fine examples of 'grandmother's cooking', but it's the desserts that really catch the eye (*Apfelstrudel*, *Sachertorte* and *Mohr im Hemd*).

Café Zilk 16

Naglerg. 11

✆ 533 4529

U-Bahn Sephansplatz

Open: Mon–Sat 0900–2100, Sun 1000–1800

€

This stylish, modern café is the first to be named after a living ex-mayor (!). The menu features Viennese breakfasts and single lunch dishes, including potato soup, mozzarella and toast and mackerel. The waiting staff speak English, and this is one of the few cafés not wreathed in cigarette smoke. Takes all credit cards.

Al Cavallino 17

Dorotheerg. 19

✆ 512 3936

U-Bahn Stephansplatz

Open: Mon–Sat 1130–1430, 1800–2300

€

A pizzeria, offering Austrian specialities as well as Italian pasta and fish dishes. The wines include a worthy Chianti Classico from the Antinori estate.

Göttweiger Stiftskeller 🔞

Spiegelg. 9

☏ 512 7817

🚇 U-Bahn Stephansplatz

Open: Mon–Thu 0800–2200, Fri 0800–2100

€–€€

A prize find, this elegant café boasts some of the best *Hausmannskost* in the city at very affordable prices. Recommended: *Tafelspitz*, *Schweinsbraten* and *Bauenschmaus*.

Herrenhof 🔞

Herreng. 10

☏ 533 5147

🚇 U-Bahn Herrengasse

Open: Mon–Fri 0700–2200, Sat 0800–1800, Sun 0800–1600

€

Attractive, spacious coffeehouse in a street of former palaces, a stone's throw from the Hofburg. Regulars come here to play cards or chess and you can watch them while mulling over a menu which includes a choice of breakfasts and traditional Viennese specials.

Il Tempo 🔞

Wallnerstr. 2

☏ 533 1895

🚇 U-Bahn Herrengasse

Open: daily 0930–2400

€

'Go with the times' is the motto of this Italian café-bistro which features a world clock in the décor. There's a choice of Tuscan wines and American cocktails to accompany the snacks, which include soups, sandwiches, salads and pasta dishes.

Kanzleramt 🔞

Schauflerg. 6

☏ 535 3945

🚇 U-Bahn Herrengasse

Open: Mon–Sat 1000–2400

€€

With a nice location on the corner of Michaelerplatz, this typical, if rather formal, *Lokal* makes a useful lunch stop if you've been tramping round the Hofburg. The cooking is Viennese and international with Styrian specialities and goulashes to the fore. Takes all credit cards.

Molly Darcy's Irish Pub 🔞

Teinfaltstr. 6

☏ 533 2311

🚇 U-Bahn Herrengasse

Open: Mon–Thu 1100–0200, Fri–Sat 1100–0300

€

Probably the best of the Irish pub bunch. Pluses include Kilkenny and Guinness on draught, TV screen for sporting events and appetising pub grub until 2200.

Naschmarkt 🔞

Schotteng. 1

☏ 533 5186

🚇 U-Bahn Schottentor

Open: Mon–Fri 1030–2100, Sat–Sun 1030–1530

€

▲ Café Griensteidl

▲ Nordsee

Busy self-service restaurant with a branch in Schwarzenbergplatz. Look for the good-value daily specials which may run out if you don't arrive early. No-smoking sections.

Nordsee 24

Kohlmarkt 6

✆ 533 5966

Ⓤ U-Bahn Stephansplatz

Open: Mon–Sat 0900–2000, Sun 1000–2000

€ – €€

This German chain of fish shops and restaurants has been around for more than 100 years. Today's branches are bright, modern, roomy and spotlessly clean. You can order from the seafood buffet, from the baguette counter or from the menu of hot dishes that include fried and baked fish, paella and soups.

Opera 25

Augustinerstr. 12

✆ 512 7159

Ⓤ U-Bahn Stephansplatz

Open: daily 1000–0200

€

Café-bar by the Hofburg serving appetising Viennese dishes, including a very moreish bacon and potato soup flavoured with wine. Draught beers include Guinness. Takes all credit cards.

Palmenhaus 26

Burggarten

✆ 533 1033

Ⓤ U-Bahn Babenbergerstrasse

Open: daily 1000–0200; hot food 1200–2400

€

The newly renovated palm house in the Burggarten is the stunning setting for this café-restaurant. The food is over-rated but there's an excellent selection of wines, a choice of international newspapers, occasional live music and a large garden with views on to the park. Breakfast is served from 1000 to 1400. (Entrance from the corner of Goethegasse and Hanuschgasse until 2000, later from Ringstrasse and the Imperial Palace gardens.)

Tricaffè 27

Bräunerstr. 4–6

✆ 535 0844

Ⓤ U-Bahn Herrengasse

Open: Mon–Sat 0800–2400, Sun 1200–2300

€€

Comfortable café-restaurant with small terrace, specialising in pizzas and Tuscan dishes, including fish. Takes all credit cards. Italian wines.

Zum Lipizzaner 28

Bräunerstr. 8

✆ 533 9091

Ⓤ U-Bahn Herrengasse

Open: Mon–Sat 1100–2400

€€

Almost next door to the famous riding school, this café-restaurant serves traditional Viennese fare – Schnitzel, goulash, pork medallions with cheese, potato soup, smoked ham, and much more besides.

HERRENGASSE
Shops, markets and picnic sites

Bakers and confectioners

Anker 29

Naglerg. 13

🚇 U-Bahn Stephansplatz

Open: Mon–Fri 0700–1800,
Sat 0800–1200

Central branch of a
major bakery chain,
founded back in
Imperial times. Apart
from bread (delivered
twice daily), there's
brioche, doughnuts,
buns, croissants, *Torten*
and strudels.

Café-Konditorei 30

Herreng. 6–8

🚇 U-Bahn Herrengasse

Open: Mon–Fri 0700–1830,
Sat 0800–1200

Pastry shop selling filled
rolls, croissants, *Torten*,
strudels and bread made
with pumpkin seeds,
olives and nuts.

Demmers Teehaus 31

Mölkerbastei 5

🚇 U-Bahn Schottentor

Open: Mon–Fri 0900–1800,
Sat 0900–1230

Two hundred and fifty
assortments of tea are
on sale here, also acces-
sories (teapots, cups,
caddies). Café upstairs.

Janele 32

Hereng. 6/Kohlmarkt 4

🚇 U-Bahn
Herrengasse/Stephansplatz

Open: Mon–Fri 0700–1830,
Sat 0800–1200

A bakery where you can
also take breakfast or
enjoy a dessert.

Groceries and supermarkets

Julius Meinl 33

Seilerg. 4

🚇 U-Bahn Herrengasse

Open: Mon–Fri 0730–1830,
Sat 0730–1500

A large branch of the
major Austrian super-
market chain. There's a
smaller shop on
Schottengasse, at the
corner of Mölker Steig.

Keck's Feine Kost 34

Herreng. 15

🚇 U-Bahn Herrengasse

Open: Mon–Fri 1000–2200,
Sat 1000–1500

Useful delicatessen with
an enticing salad
counter and Austrian
breads from the
Waldviertel and Wachau
regions. Opposite Café
Central.

Radatz 35

Schotteng. 3a

🚇 U-Bahn Schottentor-
Universität

Open: Mon–Fri 0700–1900,
Sat 0730–1300

This delicatessen and
rôtisserie has a good
range of European
cheeses: Gouda, Bel
Paese, Camembert,
Roquefort, to name a
few. Also cold meats,
salads, bread and
sandwiches to eat in or
take away.

Subway 36

Seilerg. 6

🚇 U-Bahn Stephansplatz

Open: Mon–Sat 0900–2400,
Sun 1100–2400

Subway sandwiches
with various fillings
such as roast beef,
shrimps, vegetarian,
steak and even cookies.

Trzesniewski 37

Dorotheerg. 1

🚇 U-Bahn Stephansplatz

Open: Mon–Fri 0900–1930,
Sat 0900–1300 (1800 in
season)

If you're too busy sight-
seeing to linger over
lunch, this tiny sand-
wich bar, not far from
the Hofburg, may be
just the job. Open sand-
wiches, beer and spirits
also on sale.

▲ Anker

Japanese restaurants and sushi bars

The new craze

Japanese eateries are very much the rage at the moment, with restaurants, sushi bars and noodle joints sprouting all over the place. Authentic sushi chefs don't come cheap – a master of the art must train in Japan for seven years before receiving his diploma. Sushi bars make an excellent lunch stop and aren't always as expensive as you might think. You'll often see guests sitting by a conveyor belt from which they select the dishes they want. This way of eating is known as *kaiten zushi*. Many bars (and some restaurants) offer good-value set-price meals, as well as a takeaway service (the meals are served in compartmentalised boxes called *bento*).

While most restaurants have picture menus, it may be helpful to know the names of some of the more common dishes and ingredients:

miso – traditional starter; soup comprising a thick paste of fermented soya beans

saké – a strong rice wine, usually served warm but often chilled in summer

sashimi – raw fish

shabu shabu – traditional peasant stew, composed of meat and vegetable leftovers

sushi – the generic term for any combination of raw fish, shellfish or vegetables, served with rice and a hint of the fiery green mustard known as wasabi

sushi-maki – sushi rolled inside a wrapper of dried seaweed

tempura – fish or vegetables dipped in light batter and deep fried

tepanyaki – 'grilled on an iron plate'; slices of beef, fish and vegetables are cooked at the hot plate by the chef in full view of diners

teriyaki – cooking method; the meat is marinated in *shoyu* (soy sauce and *saké*), then grilled

tofu – soya bean curd used in simmered or grilled dishes, or deep fried

udon, soba and somen – types of noodle

• **Akakiko** *Mariahilferstr. 42–8;* Ø *524 0616;* ⊕ *U-Bahn Lerchenfelderstrasse; open: daily 1100–2400;* ❷❸. Sushi, *sashimi* and *tempura* specialities are served on a roof terrace with

great views of Vienna. Menu in German and Japanese only.

• **Akashi** *Kärntnerstr. 32–34; ∅ 513 7003;* 🚇 *U-Bahn Karlsplatz; open: daily 1100–2330;* ❷❷. Small sushi bar, specialising in Californian *maki. Bento* (lunchboxes) ready to take away.

• **Busan Sushi** *Reinprechtsdorferstr. 57a; ∅ 544 3644;* 🚇 *U-Bahn Pilgramgasse; open: Mon–Sat 1130–1430, 1800–2300;* ❷❷. Sushi, *sashimi* and *tempura* with tasty seaweed specialities. Lively atmosphere.

• **Fuji** *Josefstädterstr. 9; ∅ 408 3439;* 🚇 *U-Bahn Rathaus; open: daily 1130–1430, 1730–2330; reservations unnecessary; all credit cards accepted;* ❷❷. Standard Japanese eatery with paper lantern décor and picture menus to guide the uninitiated. The fish delicacies catch the eye and include shrimp, salmon, yellowtail, horse mackerel and crab.

▲ Sushi chef, Tenmaya

You'll often see guests sitting by a conveyor belt from which they select the dishes they want.

• **Kiang Noodles** *Joanellig. 3, off Gumpendorferstr.; ∅ 586 8796;* 🚇 *U-Bahn Kettenbrückengasse; open: Mon–Sat 1800–2400; reservations unnecessary; no credit cards accepted;* ❷❷. Soups are the speciality here, as well as noodle dishes.

• **Tenmaya** *Krugerstr. 3; ∅ 512 7397;* 🚇 *U-Bahn Karlsplatz; open: daily 1130–1500, 1700–2400; reservations recommended; all credit cards accepted;* ❸❸❸. Up-market restaurant divided into three sections – *tepanyaki* grill, sushi-*sashimi* bar and formal Tatami rooms.

• **Toko-Ri** *Franz-Hochedlinder-G. 2; ∅ 214 8940;* 🚇 *trams 31 and 32; open: Mon–Sat 1200–1500, 1800–2300; reservations recommended; all credit cards accepted;* ❸❸❸. Good-value lunches and wonderful sushi make this one of the best Japanese eateries in the city.

• **Unkai** *ANA Grand Hotel, Kärntner Ring 9; ∅ 515 809110;* 🚇 *U-Bahn Karlsplatz; open: Mon 1800–2245, Tue–Sun 1200–1430 1800–2245; reservations recommended; all credit cards accepted;* ❸❸❸. Vienna's first Japanese restaurant serves a mouth-watering array of sushi, *sashimi* and *tepanyaki* dishes. The sushi-brunch (Sundays) is also worth investigating.

• **Yohm** *Yugetsu, Führichg. 10; ∅ 512 2720;* 🚇 *U-Bahn Oper; open: daily 1200–1430, 1800–2300; reservations recommended; all credit cards accepted;* ❸❸❸. The entire upper floor of the restaurant is a *tepanyaki* kitchen with shrimp specialities. Otherwise, it's sushi, *sashimi* and *tempura*, with a 'Grand Sushi-buffet' at weekends. The set-dinner menu is good value.

The Bermuda Triangle

'**B**ermuda Drei-Eck', to give it its German name, refers to the concentration of bars, restaurants and nightspots around the Ruprechtskirche. It's a quarter that only really comes alive after dark, when the clubbers and party-goers move in.

THE BERMUDA TRIANGLE
Restaurants

Capriccio da Conte ❶

Kurrentg. 1

☎ 533 6464-0

Ⓤ U-Bahn Herrengasse

Open: Mon–Sun 1200–1500, 1800–2400

Reservations recommended

All credit cards accepted

Italian

❸❸❸

The genial owner of this fairly formal Italian restaurant greets everyone with a smile. Meals here are expensive though, so if you're not in the mood to shell out, avoid the à la carte in favour of the set menu or business lunch. Dishes include a creditable *lombato di vitello tartufata* (veal in truffle sauce) and *coda di rospo al Livornese* (monkfish), though nothing is really outstanding.

Fadringer ❷

Wipplingerstr. 29

☎ 533 4341

Ⓤ U-Bahn Stephansplatz

Open: Mon–Fri 0900–2400

Reservations essential

No credit cards accepted

Viennese

❸❸❸

Small but elegant, Fadringer is currently one of Vienna's most talked about gourmet temples, with a great line in Austrian nouvelle cuisine. The set lunch here is a real bargain, although everything is excellent value for money. Recommended: veal, fish dishes and *Zwiebelrostbraten* (steak in gravy topped with onions).

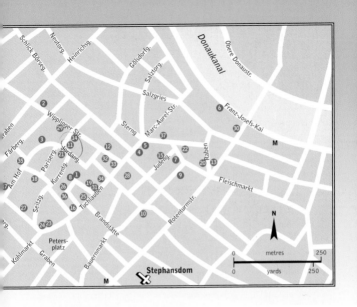

▲ Bermuda Triangle

Gustl Bauer

Drahtg. 2

☎ 533 5889

🚇 U-Bahn Herrengasse

Open: Mon–Fri 1100–2300, Sat 1100–1500

Reservations recommended

All credit cards accepted

Viennese

€€

A quaint old house on the corner of Am Hof has been extended to make more room for this traditional *Beisl*. The cooking is Viennese with Bohemian specialities, and while the food isn't particularly distinguished (or distinctive), there's a terrace overlooking the charming square.

Koh-i-Noor

Marc-Aurel-Str. 8

☎ 533 0080

🚇 U-Bahn Schwedenplatz

Open: daily 1130–1430, 1800–2300

Reservations unnecessary

All credit cards accepted

Indian

€€

Pleasant, nicely decorated restaurant specialising in North Indian cuisine: tandoori oven dishes, grills, hot and spicy *garam masala* and vegetarian meals.

Kornat

Marc-Aurel-Str. 8

☎ 535 6518

🚇 U-Bahn Schwedenplatz

Open: Mon–Sat 1130–1500, 1800–2330

Reservations recommended

Croatian

€€

Small Croatian restaurant bringing the tastes of the Dalmatian coast to landlocked Vienna. Seafood is what they do best here, but also consider the grilled fish – ask the waiter what's fresh. Wines hailing from Hvar and Korcula add authenticity to a thoroughly enjoyable experience. Speak up before you order if you're not partial to garlic!

Lale

Franz-Josefs-Kai 29

☎ 535 2736

🚇 U-Bahn Schwedenplatz

Open: daily 1130–2400

Reservations recommended

No credit cards accepted

Turkish

€€

A stone's throw from the bars and nightspots of the Bermuda Triangle, this busy but relaxed Turkish restaurant is a cut above most in the city. Arty photographs decorate the plain white walls while the main dining space overlooks the kitchen so you can see what the chef's up to! Friendly staff are happy to advise on the choice of *mezes* (starters). Main courses include a heavenly Adana kebab special, cooked over a wood-fired grill, then served with lashings of tomato and yoghurt dressing.

Mongolian Barbecue

Fleischmarkt 4, 1st Floor

☎ 535 3176

🚇 U-Bahn Schwedenplatz

Open: daily 1200–1500, 1730–2330

Reservations recommended

All credit cards accepted

Mongolian

€€

This upstairs restaurant advertises outside number four. The main feature is the set price Mongolian grill buffet, comprising vegetables, meat and seafood, with large helpings of salad. Children aged six to nine go half price. Drinks are charged separately. There's an open grill so you can watch the chef at work, but this isn't the kind of place where you'd want to spend all evening.

Ofenloch

Kurrentg. 8

☎ 533 8844

🚇 U-Bahn Herrengasse

Open: daily 1000–2400

Reservations recommended

All credit cards accepted

Viennese

€€€

This homely, beautifully decorated *Beisl* in the

heart of the Altstadt dates back to 1704. The Austrian term *gemütlich* (cosy, agreeable) describes it to a 'T', though the number of tourists is beginning to scare off the locals. Viennese home cooking is the chef's forte.

Rosa Elefant

Bauernmarkt 21

✆ 533 7530

Ⓤ U-Bahn Schwedenplatz

Open: Mon–Sat 1800–0200, Sun 1600–2400

Reservations recommended

All credit cards accepted

Viennese

€€

The menu in this dark, wood-panelled *Lokal* changes every week – meat for the most part, although there are always a couple of vegetarian dishes available. A mainly young clientele, attracted no doubt by the late opening (kitchen closes 0045) and the proximity of the Bermuda Triangle, tucks in to hearty platefuls of *Beinfleisch*, *Tafelspitz* and the like.

Wrenkh ⑩

Bauernmarkt 10

✆ 533 1526

Ⓤ U-Bahn Stephansplatz

Open: daily 1100–2400

Reservations recommended

All credit cards accepted

Vegetarian

€€€

Vienna's leading vegetarian restaurant is on the pricey side but the cooking is resourceful and creative. The à la carte menu is extensive and wide-ranging and there's a set menu and lunch specials through-out the week, with Sunday brunch from 1130 until 1600. The waiting staff are courteous and helpful and there's a nice, relaxed atmosphere. Specialities include salads and wild mushroom risotto.

Zum Scherer ⑪

Judenpl. 7

✆ 533 5164

Ⓤ U-Bahn Herrengasse

Open: Mon–Sat 1100–0100, Sun 1700–2400

Reservations unnecessary

No credit cards accepted

Austrian

€–€€

This *Beisl* with a quaint location in the historic Jewish quarter has a contemporary feel, notwithstanding the old-world façade. While the focus is on traditional Austrian dishes, there's a strong Hungarian influence at work in the kitchen, and a commendable striving for authenticity. Recommended: cabbage soup, Budapest pork cutlet, pike-perch from Lake Balaton.

THE BERMUDA TRIANGLE
Bars, cafés and pubs

Altes Rathauskeller

Wipplingerstr. 8

✆ 535 3336

Ⓤ U-Bahn Stephansplatz

Open: Mon–Sat 1130–1430, 1730–2330; closed Sat Jul–Aug

€€

Pretty basic Viennese cooking in the cellar of the Old Town Hall. The eclectic menu ranges from roasted veal liver to pancakes.

Bermuda Bräu 🝢

Rabensteig 6

✆ 532 2865

Ⓤ U-Bahn Schwedenplatz

Open: daily 1100–0200

€

Lively pub in the heart of the much-hyped Bermuda Triangle. The sound system can be ear-splitting, but the pub grub, with Tex-Mex influences, is acceptable enough and available until the small hours. Beer is served in tankards (*Tonkrugen*).

Bieradies 🝣

Judenpl. 1

✆ 535 6611

Ⓤ U-Bahn Stephansplatz

Open: Mon–Sat 1100–0200

€–€€

Near the controversial new Holocaust memorial, the main draw here is the beer which comes from the Villach brewery on the Wörthersee. It goes hand in hand with the Carinthian dessert: baked apple with cherries and cinnamon. Otherwise it's the Mexican dishes, jalapeño peppers, burritos, and so on, that catch the eye.

Café Boheme 🝥

Judeng. 5

✆ 535 5649

Ⓤ U-Bahn Schwedenplatz

Open: Mon–Sat 1100–0200, Sun 1800–0200

€

Tequila bar on the fringes of the Bermuda Triangle, also serving American Budweiser on draught. Happy hour 1700 to 1800.

Café Tuchlauben 🝦

Tuchlauben 16

✆ 533 4136

Ⓤ U-Bahn Stephansplatz

Open: Mon–Fri 0700–1800

€

One of Vienna's better-known coffeehouses, the only sound you'll hear in Tuchlauben is the rustling of newspapers. While the décor is charmless, the home-made desserts are a bargain, as is the chicken soup and other snacks.

È tricaffe 🝧

Am Hof 2

✆ 533 8490

Ⓤ U-Bahn Herrengasse

Open: Mon–Sat 0800–2400, Sun 1000–2400

€€

The Tuscan specialities created by chef Herbert Malek won high marks in a recent survey. Try any of the delectable *antipasti*, or make do with a sandwich, if you haven't time to linger. Also on sale are Tuscan olive oils and coffees.

Gösser Bierklinik 🝨

Steindlg. 4

✆ 535 6897

Ⓤ U-Bahn Schwedenplatz

Open: Mon–Sat 1000–2300

€€

This rambling building dates back to the year 1566. As the name implies, beer from the Gösser brewery in Styria is the speciality, though you can also eat lunch – try the Tyrolean dish known as *Gröstl* (pan-fried meat and potato). One of the dining rooms is for non-smokers – unusual in Vienna.

Kolar 🔟

Kleeblattg. 5

☎ 533 5225

Ⓤ U-Bahn Stephansdplatz

Open: daily 1700–0200

€

Popular *Beisl* selling pub grub cooked on a wood-fired grill. The draught beers include Hirter, Budweiser-Budvar, Wieselburger, and Puntigammer Panther.

Krah Krah 🔢

Rabensteig 8

☎ 533 8193

Ⓤ U-Bahn Schwedenplatz

Open: daily 1100–0200

€

The first pub in the Bermuda Triangle, Krah Krah remains especially popular with students and young people, though any beer enthusiast is welcome. Kulmbach and Guinness are just two of umpteen world brews on offer, and the Viennese snacks too are worth getting to grips with. Live music at weekends, including jazz. Happy hour is 1530 until 1730 Monday to Friday.

Panther Bräu 🔢

Judenpl. 9–10

☎ 533 4426

Ⓤ U-Bahn Stephansplatz

Open: Mon–Fri 1000–2300

€–€€

This charming pub, opposite the old Bohemian chancellery, offers hearty Viennese fare and excellent

▲ Zum Schwarzen Kameel

beer – Puntigammer Panther – on draught. Terrace seating on the square in summer.

Zum Kuchldragoner 🔢

Seitenstetteng. 3/Ruprechtspl. 4–5

☎ 533 8371

Ⓤ U-Bahn Schwedenplatz

Open: daily 1100–0400

€€

Modernish *Beisl* with terrace seating behind the Ruprechtskirche. Great atmosphere and the meals here are good value.

Zum Schwarzen Kameel 🔢

Bognerg. 5

☎ 533 8967

Ⓤ U-Bahn Herrengasse

Open: Mon–Fri 0830–2030, Sat 0830–1630

€€–€€€

Well-known deli and wine shop with an attractive Jugendstil restaurant upstairs, designed by Adolf Loos. Sandwiches, snacks and more formal meals are beautifully prepared and great value. The service too is impeccable.

THE BERMUDA TRIANGLE
Shops, markets and picnic sites

Aida 24

Bognerg. 3

🔵 U-Bahn Herrengasse

Open: Mon–Sat 0630–1900,
Sun 0900–1900

A *Café-Konditorei* selling chocolates as well as cakes. Look out for Viennese specialities such as *Himbeerstangel* (raspberry jam turnover) and *Biedermeiertorte*. Some indoor seating, but smoky.

Auer Brot 25

Tuchlauben 20

🔵 U-Bahn Stephansplatz

Open: Mon–Fri 0900–1800,
Sat 0900–1300

A tiny modern bakery specialising in Viennese, Styrian and other regional breads.

Bäckerei Grimm 26

Kurrentg. 10

🔵 U-Bahn Stephansplatz

Open: Mon–Fri 0900–1800,
Sat 0900–1300

Neighbourhood bakery with an amusing selection of novelty breads (clowns, faces, and so on). All bread is freshly baked on the premises.

City Confisserie 27

Bognerg. 5

🔵 U-Bahn Herrengasse

Open: Mon–Fri 0800–1900,
Sat 0900–1700

Colourful window displays are the hallmark of this sweet shop. Apart from the marzipan chocolates known as *Mozartkugeln*, you'll find nougat, peppermint, jellies and *Kieselsteinen* ('pebble stones').

Gelateria Italiano 28

Hoher Markt 4

🔵 U-Bahn Stephansplatz

Open: daily 0900–2330

Genuine Italian ice-cream parlour with more than 24 flavours to choose from. Strawberry is a house speciality.

Karl Haag 29

Wipplingerstr. 6

🔵 U-Bahn Stephansplatz

Open: Mon–Fri 0800–1800

If you're in the vicinity of the Old Town Hall (Altes Rathaus) you may want to call in at this well-known *Café-Konditorei* for an Austrian coffee and pastry. Bread and cakes are also on sale.

Der Mann 30

Rotenturmstr. 1/Stehrhof

🔵 U-Bahn Schwedenplatz

Open: Mon–Fri 0900–1800,
Sat 0900–1300

Tyrolean pumpkin-seed bread is the speciality here. The displays of croissants, filled rolls and pastries are equally enticing.

Perpizzolo KEG 31

Tuchlauben 15

🔵 U-Bahn Stephansplatz

Open: daily 0930–2330

Ice-cream specialists: among the more unusual flavours are cranberry and nougat. Limited terrace seating.

Aibler 32

Wipplingerstr. 3

🔵 U-Bahn Stephansplatz

Open: Mon–Fri 0800–1800

This august delicatessen was founded back in 1911. The meat and cheese counter will take your breath away. Fill up on rolls, soups and light snacks such as roast meat with salad.

Biowein & Design 33

Wipplingerstr. 1

🔵 U-Bahn Stephansplatz

Open: Mon–Fri 1000–1830,
Sat 1000–1700

Organic wines from Austria, France and Italy, and designer accessories.

Champagnerie ③④

Kleeblattg. 13

🔘 U-Bahn Stephansplatz

Open: Mon–Sat 1700–2400

This outlet is the sole importer of 'Riesener' champagne and describes itself as a boutique. Magnums as well as bottles.

Sankt Urban Weinhandlung ③⑤

Am Hof 11, corner of Heidenschuss

🔘 U-Bahn Herrengasse

Open: Mon–Fri 0900–1900, Sat 1000–1400.

This wine trader's has been in business since 1683 and occupies the site of an old inn. Showcase for vintage wines of every description, including champagnes.

Wlaschitz ③⑥

Kurrentg. 10

🔘 U-Bahn Herrengasse

Open: Tue 1700–2100, Thu 1700–2100, Fri 1300–1800, Sat 0900–1300

Specialist in Austrian wines: Blaufränkisch, Rheinriesling, Grüner Veltiner and St Laurent.

Zum Finsteren Stern ③⑦

Sterng. 2

🔘 U-Bahn Schwedenplatz

Open: Mon–Fri 1600–2400, Sat 1430–2100

Wine tastings are offered prior to purchase, or you can linger and imbibe on the premises like the locals. The wine bar is an attractive *Lokal* with wooden floorboards, chests of drawers and crates of empties lying about the place.

▲ Aida

Prater

Vienna's playground

This famous public park was presented to the people of Vienna in 1766 by Emperor Josef II; it was originally an Imperial game reserve. Today it's best known for the sprawling amusement park at the western end, known as the Wurstel or Volksprater. This traditional funfair has everything – more than 200 booths, a ghost train, dodgem and go-kart rides, a merry-go-round, a hall of mirrors, slides, shooting galleries and a miniature railway (the **Liliputbahn**). Towering above the site is the **Riesenrad**, a giant Ferris wheel constructed by English engineers at the end of the 19th century and still in good working order. It's 65 metres high and there are panoramic views over Vienna and the Danube from the cabins. One of the most famous scenes from the 1949 classic movie *The Third Man* (starring Orson Welles) was filmed on the ride. The Prater also features in the 15th James Bond movie, *The Living Daylights*, made in 1987.

You can explore the woods and meadows by following any of the paths which criss-cross the park. The main avenue, or Hauptallee, is 5 kilometres long and was laid out in the 18th century. The **Planetarium** is at the end nearest Praterstern U-Bahn station. Other attractions in the Prater include a swimming pool (Stadionbad), a golf course, tennis courts, a trotting stadium and a race track, so there really is something here for everyone.

The Prater is the perfect spot for picnicking, but if you prefer to let others do the cooking you'll find everything here, from hot dog stalls to beer gardens and conventional restaurants.

• **Altes Jägerhaus** *Freudenau 255; ∅ 728 9577; open: Apr–Sept daily 0900–2300, Oct–Mar Wed–Sun 0900–2300; ❷❷.* Situated at the far end of the Hauptallee and surrounded by woods and meadows, the 'Old Hunting Lodge' has a large garden with plenty of shade in the summer. The old-fashioned Viennese cooking

▲ Riesenrad

uses tried and tested family recipes.

• **Liane Neumüller** *Prater 28; ✆ 728 0083; open: daily 0900– 2300;* ❻❻. Located near the main entrance to the park, this roomy restaurant offers Viennese dishes and traditional specialities, plus an impressive beer and wine cellar. Shady garden.

• **Schweizerhaus** *Prater 116; ✆ 728 0152; open: Mar–Oct daily 1000–2300;* ❻❻–❻❻❻. Around 100,000 diners flock to the Schweizerhaus each year, so come early if you want to be sure of a table. The restaurant (founded in 1920) has a huge garden which attracts a lively mix of Viennese businessmen, daytrippers and foreign visitors. The waiters rush about with frothy tankards of Budweiser-Budvar and gargantuan joints of pork. The menu includes dishes from all over the former Austro-Hungarian Empire: *čevapčiči* from Serbia, *Pusztaschnitzel* from Hungary, *Krautsuppe* from Slovakia, *Powidltascherl* from Bohemia, and so on. You can also order Viennese classics, including *Backhendl*, *Apfelstrudel* and the house speciality, *Schweinsstelze* (pigs' trotters).

• **Wieselburger Bierinsel** *Prater 11; ✆ 729 4785; open: daily 0830– 2300 (kitchen from 1100);* ❻❻❻. The 'Beer Island' offers international as well as Austrian dishes (including fish), homemade cakes, ice creams and a choice of seven draught beers. There's a traditional country buffet on Tuesday

▲ Schweizerhaus

evenings and an Italian buffet on Thursdays. If you're really famished, go for the grilled pigs' trotters – with all the trimmings, naturally. Large garden area, non-smoking section.

• **Zum 'Englischen Reiter'** *Str. des Ersten Mai 58; ✆ 728 0759; open: daily 0900–2300;* ❻❻–❻❻❻. This large, family-run restaurant is in the heart of the park. The homely fare includes pork steak, served on a platter with French fries and vegetables, bacon and eggs, and so on. Live music performances take place in the spacious garden, weather permitting, and there's a roofed playground for the youngsters.

> You'll find everything here, from hot dog stalls to beer gardens and conventional restaurants.

• **Zum Wilden Mann** *Prater 4; ✆ 729 4786; open: mid-Mar–mid-Nov daily 1100–2200;* ❻–❻❻. This country restaurant and beer cellar is especially popular with beer enthusiasts as it produces its own brews. The large garden has a children's play area.

• **Prater** Ⓤ *U-Bahn Praterstern; open: funfair – Apr–Oct daily (times vary), Ferris wheel – Feb–Nov and New Year daily, swimming pool – May–Sept daily, miniature railway – Apr–mid-Oct daily.*

Fleischmarkt

Back in the 13th century this area was the city's meat market, hence the name. The eateries still have a cosmopolitan flavour, reflecting a long tradition of immigration.

FLEISCHMARKT
Restaurants

Achilleus ❶

Köllnerhofg. 3

∅ 512 8328

Ⓜ U-Bahn Stephansplatz

Open: daily 1130–1430, 1700–0030 (evenings only in summer)

Reservations recommended

All credit cards accepted

Greek

❷❸

Prompt service and tasty Greek food are the hallmarks of this friendly eatery. The *stifado* and the calamari are especially good, and the pseudo-rustic décor creates a cheerful ambience. There's a stand-up counter (*Imbiss*) offering a similar menu at Fleischmarkt 22 – 'Achilleus Box'.

Artemis ❷

Griecheng. 3

∅ 525 4169

Ⓜ U-Bahn Schwedenplatz

Open: Mon–Sat 1700–2400, Sun 1200–1500, 1700–2400

Reservations recommended

All credit cards accepted

Greek

❷❸

Greek and Levantine communities settled around the Fleischmarkt in the 17th century, or even earlier. This large restaurant, sporting the national colours of blue and white, is near the Greek church. The seafood (calamari, scampi) is good here, or there's a special fish platter. Meat dishes include moussaka and a spicy *souvlaki* (lamb grilled on a skewer). *Skordalia* (garlic dip) goes down a treat with the traditional flatbread

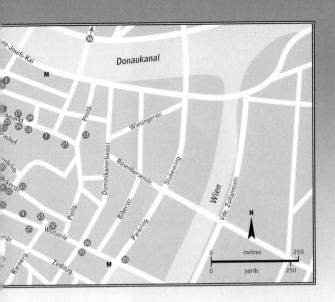

and makes a good starter.

Cavaliere ❺

Köllnerhofg. 4

✆ 513 8320

Ⓤ U-Bahn Stephansplatz

Open: daily 1130–2330

Reservations recommended

All credit cards accepted

Italian

❶❶

Tasty, filling pizzas baked in the traditional wood-burning oven and a creditable choice of Italian wines – Chianti Classico, Brunello di Montalcino, Bardolino and Barolo – are the strong points of this pleasant, if unexciting, trattoria.

Figlmüller ❹

Wollzeile 5

✆ 512 6177

Ⓤ U-Bahn Stephansplatz

Open: daily 1100–2230

Reservations unnecessary

▨

Viennese

❶❶

The main entrance to this fabled *Stadtheurige* is in the shopping arcade known as Wollzeile Passage. The glass terrace is liable to be full to bursting, but so are the tiny inside rooms – tell the waiter you'd like a table and he'll collect you from

▲ Figlmüller Wiener Schnitzel

the wine bar opposite when they're ready. Ignore whatever else is on the menu and make a beeline for the Wiener Schnitzel – they don't come any bigger or better than here. The wine (served in jugs) comes from Figlmüller's own vineyard in Grinzing (*see page 80*).

Griechenbeisl

Fleischmarkt 11

✆ 533 1977

🚇 U-Bahn Schwedenplatz

Open: daily 1100–0100

Reservations unnecessary

No credit cards accepted

Viennese

💰💰💰

The oldest inn in Vienna, Griechenbeisl opened in 1477 as 'The Yellow Eagle' – it was given its present name after the Turkish siege, when the Greek community settled in the area – their descendants still worship in the Orthodox church next door. Beethoven, Schubert and Brahms all supped in the cosy panelled rooms, now crammed with tourists who are charged rather more than the going rate for what is pretty standard Viennese fare. Console yourself with a glass or two of the Czech beer, Pilsner Urquell – the landlord was the first to introduce the delectable brew to Vienna soon after its launch in 1852.

Kornhäuslturm ⑥

Fleischmarkt 1a

✆ 535 5936

🚇 U-Bahn Schwedenplatz

Open: daily 1130–2200

Reservations recommended

All credit cards accepted

Viennese

💰💰

This family-run restaurant near the old meat market offers reasonably priced set menus for lunch and dinner during the week and at lunchtimes on weekends. Typical dishes include French onion soup with cheese toast, venison ragout, chicken breast stuffed with asparagus and mixed salad with curd cheese and cream. If you can't find a table within the designated non-smoking area, it can be a bit stuffy here. Small terrace.

Maredo ⑦

Fleischmarkt 18

✆ 512 5729

🚇 U-Bahn Schwedenplatz

Open: daily 1130–2400

Reservations unnecessary

All credit cards accepted

South American

💰💰

Latest branch of a German-owned restaurant chain. The Latin American specialities range from steaks and grills to *tapas*, soups, ribs and seafood, also platters and combinations. Salad bar, children's portions, large no-smoking area and occasional live music.

Pfudl 8

Bäckerstr. 22

✆ 512 6705

Ⓤ U-Bahn Stephansplatz

Open: Mon–Sat 0900–0200, Sun 0900–1500

Reservations recommended

All credit cards accepted

Austrian

❸❸

One of Vienna's leading *Beisln*, Pfudl has a reputation for excellent *Hausmannskost* (home cooking), though some of the meals can be a bit on the heavy side. English is one of several languages spoken here so you can rely on someone to guide you through the menu and point you in the direction of the salad bar. There's a wine of the month as well as draught beer. Viennese music.

Plachutta 9

Wollzeile 38

✆ 512 1577

Ⓤ U-Bahn Stubentor

Open: daily 1130–2315

Reservations recommended

All credit cards accepted

Austrian

❸❸

Plachutta Junior is the chef at this restaurant in the *Wirtshaus* tradition, showcasing prime quality beef from Styria. For these reasons, it's the ideal place to sample Emperor Franz-Josef's favourite, *Tafelspitz*. *Beinfleisch* is the other speciality. Bright décor but the atmosphere is a bit on the formal side.

Siddhartha 10

Fleischmarkt 16

✆ 513 1197

Ⓤ U-Bahn Schwedenplatz

Open: Mon 1130–1500, Tue–Sat 1130–1500, 1800–2300

Reservations recommended

All credit cards accepted

Vegetarian

❸❸

This informal restaurant in the Buddhist centre is a real find, and not only if you're a vegetarian. Flowers and candles help to create a wonderfully relaxed atmosphere in which to ponder the extensive menu. One highlight is the *Indische Traum* (Indian Dream), a plate of different curries with samosa, chapatis and chutneys. The artichoke pizza is equally delectable, not to mention spinach Florentine with fried egg and cheese, sesame salad, flambéed tofu, broccoli medallions, nut steaks … Note that the entrance is along a passageway.

▲ Griechenbeisl

FLEISCHMARKT
Bars, cafés and pubs

Alt Wien ⑪

Bäckerstr. 9

✆ 512 5222

Ⓜ U-Bahn Stephansplatz

Open: Sun–Thu 1000–0200,
Fri–Sat 1000–0400

€

Popular late-night *Szene*
('in' bar), the haunt of
artists and left-leaning
politicos. Excellent pub
grub, including goulash,
cheese on toast, ham
and eggs, *Bohnensuppe*,
Schnitzels and home-
made cakes. Gräflich
Clamsches beers.

Bizi ⑫

Rotenturmstr. 4

✆ 513 3705

Ⓜ U-Bahn Stephansplatz

Open: daily 1100–2330

€€

One of a chain of pizze-
rias, this branch near
Stephansdom has a
large self-service salad
bar. Pasta dishes and
grilled meats also avail-
able. Takeaway service.

Café Engländer ⑬

Postg. 2

✆ 512 2734

Ⓜ U-Bahn Stubentor

Open: Mon–Sat 0800–0200,
Sun 1000–0200

€

This roomy coffeehouse
was completely

re-vamped some years
ago and given a new
lease of life. Retreat to
the terrace if you find
the smoky atmosphere a
bit much. The Viennese
cooking is pretty basic.

Capt'n Cook ⑭

Griecheng. 1

✆ 535 4483-20

Ⓜ U-Bahn Schwedenplatz

Open: Mon–Sat 1800–0200

€–€€

Model ships, flags and
pennants adorn this
nautical bar near
Fleischmarkt. You can
choose from 70 kinds of
whisky, including the
local Waldviertler. The
food is typical pub grub
– everything from club
sandwiches to fried
onion rings and
pancakes.

Daniel Moser ⑮

Rotenturmstr. 14

✆ 513 2823

Ⓜ U-Bahn Stephansplatz

Open: daily 0800–2400

€€

It was on this spot in
1685 that the Emperor
Leopold I permitted
Johann Diodato to open
Vienna's first
'Thürkischen Gethränks
Chava', or coffeehouse.
Today you can also buy
Viennese breakfast,
simple snacks and fresh
fruit juices.

▲ Bizi

Diglas 16

Wollzeile 10/Fleischmarkt 16

☎ 512 5765/512 5763-35

🚇 U-Bahn Stephansplatz

Open: Mon–Wed 0700–2330, Thu–Sat 0700–0100, Sun 0800–2330

€€

Formal and restrained, Diglas was the favourite haunt of the operetta composer Franz Léhar. Breakfast (served 0700–1100) includes ham and eggs and other delights, and Viennese specialities such as cold *Tafelspitz* salad are served at lunch.

Erdinger 17

Fleischmarkt 9

☎ 533 2873

🚇 U-Bahn Schwedenplatz

Open: Mon–Sat 1100–0100

€€

Pub with an elegant 17th-century façade and a sculpture of the Virgin and Child in a niche on the 1st floor. Erdinger Weissbier is the speciality here, but there's Budweiser export if you prefer. Lunch specialities include herring salad, salmon with noodles, pork medallions, spinach and gorgonzola.

Der Franzose 18

Sonnenfelsg. 17

☎ 513 6853

🚇 U-Bahn Stephansplatz

Open: daily 1600–0400

€€

French bistro with a small menu, including quiche Lorraine, onion soup, cheese platter and baguettes. French and Austrian wines available including champagnes.

George and the Dragon 19

Rotenturmstr. 24

☎ 533 1998

🚇 U-Bahn Schwedenplatz

Open: Mon–Sat 1000–0100

€–€€

English-style pub-restaurant and steakhouse. The desserts include the classic *Mohr im Hemd*, pancakes and strudels. Kilkenny on draught; children's meals on request; terrace seating.

MAK-Café 20

Stubenring 5

☎ 714 0121

🚇 U-Bahn Stubentor

Open: Tue–Sun 1000–0200

€–€€

This stylish café, designed by eminent architect Hermann Czech, is part of the Museum of Applied Arts (MAK in German). The quality of the food leaves something to be desired, but there's plenty of choice – vegetarian and pasta dishes as well as meat. The garden is open in summer.

Palatschinken-pfandl 21

Grashofg. 4

☎ 513 8218

🚇 U-Bahn Schwedenplatz

Open: daily 1000–2400

€–€€

As the name implies, this friendly, rather

old-fashioned café-restaurant outfit specialises in pancakes (sweet and savoury) but you'll also find plenty of international alternatives. Outdoor seating.

Vino Nobile 22

Bäckerstr. 10

☎ 513 5144

🚇 U-Bahn Stephansplatz

Open: Tue–Sat 1700–2400

€€

Homely Italian eatery offering a predictable range of good-value *antipasti* and pasta dishes. Not much room.

Weibel's 23

Riemerg. 1–3

☎ 513 3110

🚇 U-Bahn Stephansplatz

Open: Mon–Fri 0900–0030, Sat 1700–0030

€€

Tucked away in the Wollzeile passage, this branch of the Weibel chain describes itself as a bistro. As it's small and trendy, you may have to wait for a table. The menu is eclectic and includes hot and cold *tapas*, American and Viennese breakfasts and a range of *Würstel*. The Austrian wines hail from the Wachau and southern Styria.

FLEISCHMARKT
Shops, markets and picnic sites

Bakers and confectioners	

Aida 24

Wollzeile 28/Rotenturmstr. 24

Ⓜ U-Bahn Stephansplatz

Open: Mon–Sat 0630–2000, Sun 0900–2000

Popular bakery chain. Also on sale are cakes (including Biedermeier and Sacher *Torten*), sandwiches, pastries and chocolate novelties.

Bonbons 25

Wollzeile 26

Ⓜ U-Bahn Stubentor

Open: Mon–Fri 0830–1830, Sat 0900–1900, Sun 1400–1900

An Aladdin's cave for the sweet-toothed. Baskets of nougat, caramels, truffles, almond desserts and chocolates, including *Mozartkugeln*. Also 'Danube Stones' and other flights of fancy.

Eissalon 26

Dr Karl Lueger-Pl. 2

Ⓜ U-Bahn Stubentor

Open: Mon–Fri 1000–2000, Sat 0900–2000

Convenient for the Stadtpark, this ice-cream parlour also sells strudels and cakes.

Felber 27

Wollzeile 23/Fleischmarkt 28

Ⓜ U-Bahn Stubentor/ U-Bahn Schwedenplatz

Open: Mon–Fri 0630–1830, Sat 0700–1300

Baker's and confectioner's where you can buy delicious spinach strudel as well as cakes and pastries.

Heiner 28

Wollzeile 9

Ⓜ U-Bahn Stubentor

Open: Mon–Sat 0830–1900, Sun 1000–1900

Elegant confectioner's selling an appealing range of pastries and desserts. A good place to try *Guglhupf*, *Linzer Torte*, *Blumentopf*, *Trüffelkugel* and other Viennese delights.

Rosenauer 29

Fleischmarkt 12

Ⓜ U-Bahn Schwedenplatz

Open: Mon–Fri 0900–1300, 1400–1800, Sat 0900–1300

Tiny confectionery store, packed to the rafters with eminent brands of chocolates, including Lindt and Hofbau of Vienna, also pralines, *Baumküchen*, *Mozartkugeln* and nougat, to name but a few.

Ströck 30

Rotenturmstr. 8

Ⓜ U-Bahn Stephansplatz

Open: Mon–Fri 0630–1900, Sat 0700–1800, Sun 0900–1800

Bread specialities, including sunflower-seed loaves; also delicious Austrian doughnuts (*Krapfen*) and *Buchteln* (jam buns).

Zanoni & Zanoni 31

Am Lugeck 7

Ⓜ U-Bahn Stephansplatz

Open: daily 0730–2400

Huge, brightly lit ice-cream parlour with an ample no-smoking area. Thirty flavours of ice cream sold in cones or tubs, also profiteroles and pancakes.

Grocers and supermarkets	

Böhle 32

Wollzeile 30

Ⓜ U-Bahn Stubentor

Open: Mon–Fri 0830–1900, Sat 0830–1700

Delicatessen where, apart from the usual range of pâtés and preserves, you'll find Austrian wines, Blandys port, Madeira wine, liqueurs and beers from around the world – Castlemaine, Labats, Rolling Rock, Samuel

Adams, Melbourne, New York New York, Miller, Efes, and many more.

Johann Schönbichler (Teehandlung) ㉝

Wollzeile 4

Ⓤ U-Bahn Stubentor

Open: Mon–Fri 0830–1800, Sat 0830–1230

You'll find this tea importers next door to the cathedral and Diocesan museum. The teas are from around the world and you can buy gift-wrapped packages as well as caddies, teapots, and so on. Schönbichler is also a major whisky importer, as you'll notice from the amazing window displays.

Richter (Fleisch und Würst) ㉞

Fleischmarkt 17

Ⓤ U-Bahn Schwedenplatz

Open: Mon–Fri 0830–1900, Sat 0830–1700

Excellent butcher's and delicatessen with specialities such as Tiroler *Speck* and Hungarian salami. Brusque staff.

Der Teeladen ㉟

Dr Karl-Lueger-Pl. 2

Ⓤ U-Bahn Stubentor

Open: Mon–Fri 0900–1900, Sat 0900–1700

Everything connected with tea and tea making: pots, caddies, caskets, samovars, porcelain cups.

| Picnic sites |

㊱ This part of the city is fairly built up, but if you take the underground from Schwedenplatz to Volksprater (2 stops) you will have crossed the Danube Canal to arrive at the edge of the huge Prater Park (*see* *page 46*).

▲ Prater Park

Austrian cuisine

A European melting-pot

The diversity of Austrian cooking often surprises first-time visitors. Each of the eight regions produces its own culinary specialities for which the restaurants of Vienna are a showcase. Austria's geographical location at the heart of Europe and Vienna's historic role as the capital of a multi-ethnic empire account for this embarrassment of riches. Even the quintessentially 'Austrian' dish Wiener Schnitzel originated in northern Italy, where it is still known as *piccata alla Milanese*. From Hungary, via the province of **Burgenland**, come *Gulasch* (meat stew), *Letscho* (stewed tomatoes, green peppers and spices) and the sweet pancakes known as *Palatschinken*. **Styria** has its own distinctive dishes – pumpkin soup (*Kürbiskremsuppe*), *Sterz* (a corn hash originating in Slovenia) and *Würzelfleisch* (root vegetable stew). Some **Serbian** specialities, for example, *Bohnensuppe* (bean soup) and *čevapčiči* (kebab, rissole), also appear on Styrian menus. With equal resourcefulness, **Carinthia**

borrowed ravioli from the Italians to come up with *Kasnudeln* (cheese-filled pasta), while **Upper Austria**, or 'dumpling land' as it's affectionately known, owes this gastronomic delight to neighbouring **Bohemia**. Some dishes have no obvious provenance – *Tiroler Gröstl* (fried potato, meat and vegetables), for example, or *Salzburger Nockerl*, Mozart's favourite dessert long after moving to Vienna.

• **Bei Max** *Landhausg. 2; ✆ 533 7359;* 🚇 *U-Bahn Herrengasse; open: Mon–Fri 1100–2300; reservations recommended; all credit cards accepted; Carinthian-Austrian;* ❷❸. This is a cosy, wood-panelled *Lokal* that's won prizes for its quality Austrian cooking. Carinthian specialities such as *Gailtaler Kirchtagssuppe* (sour cream soup) and *Kärntner Kasnudeln* go hand in hand with such Viennese favourites as *Tafelspitz*.

• **Beim Czaak** *Postg. 15; ✆ 513 7215;* 🚇 *U-Bahn Stubentor; open: Mon–Fri 0830–2400, Sat 1100–2400; reservations recommended; all credit cards accepted; Austrian;* ❷❸. The traditional, no-frills cooking of this old-fashioned, family-run *Beisl* features Bohemian, Hungarian and Viennese specialities. Some outside seating in summer.

• **Brezl-Gwölb** *Ledererhof 9; ✆ 533 8811;* 🚇 *U-Bahn*

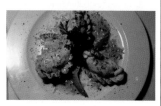

▲ *Kasnudeln*, Beim Czaak

Herrengasse; open: daily 1130–0100; reservations essential; all credit cards accepted; Austrian; ❷❸. A bakery in medieval times, this cosy little restaurant is still lit mainly by candlelight and well suited to a romantic dinner *à deux*. The menu includes regional specialities such as *Tiroler Gröstl* and *Kasnockerln*, as well as traditional Viennese dishes.

• **Kardos**
Dominikanerbastei 8; ✆ 512 6949; ⓜ *U-Bahn Stubentor; open: Mon–Sat 1000–1430, 1730–2230, Sun 1000–1700; reservations recommended; all credit cards accepted; Hungarian;* ❷❸. Kardos offers an authentic Magyar experience. Apart from the *Szegindiner Gulyas* there's fillet of pike-perch (*Fogosch*), salmon and beef steak *à la Ferencz*. Choice of Hungarian wines, pseudo-rustic décor and a welcoming staff.

• **Laterndl** *Landesgerichtsstr. 12; ✆ 409 9565;* ⓜ *U-Bahn Rathaus; open: Mon 1130–1430, Tue–Fri 1130–1430, 1800–2330, Sat 1800–2330; reservations recommended; all credit cards accepted; Austrian;* ❷❸. Laterndl has all the hallmarks of a traditional Viennese tavern, inside and out. Staff and regulars are friendly and the home cooking is the real McCoy. As well as the predictable goulashes and *Tafelspitz*, you can try regional specialities such as *Würzelfleisch*, *Gröstel* and Serbian carp fillet.

• **Mohninsel** *Florianig. 1; ✆ 403 6404;* ⓜ *U-Bahn Rathaus; open:*

... Salzburger Nockerl, Mozart's favourite dessert long after moving to Vienna ...

Mon–Sat 1100–1500, 1800–2300; reservations recommended; all credit cards accepted; Austrian; ❷❸. The rustic interior is intended to suggest Austria's Waldviertel, a lovely area of rolling countryside near the Czech border. The chef specialises in river fish (carp and pike, for example), which are coated with ground poppy seeds (*Mohn*).

• **Steirereck**
Rasumofskyg. 2; ✆ 713 3268; ⓜ *U-Bahn Rochusgasse; open: Mon–Fri 1200–1500, 1900–2400; reservations essential; all credit cards accepted; Viennese-Styrian;* ❷❸❹. It's definitely worth the trek to Landstrasse to sample the culinary magic of this fabulous restaurant, awarded top marks in a recent round-up in *Der Kurier*. 'New Viennese' cuisine is given a fascinating Styrian twist by master-chef, Helmut Österreicher. While the à la carte is predictably expensive, the set lunch menu, though not cheap, is excellent value. Winter garden.

• **Steirische Jagastubn**
Landesgerichtsstr. 12; ✆ 405 6133; ⓜ *U-Bahn Rathaus; open: Mon–Fri 1000–2400; reservations unnecessary; no credit cards accepted; Austrian;* ❷❸. Cheap and cheerful neighbourhood restaurant, rustling up good-value Styrian home cooking, including *Heidenstersuppe*, cheese dumplings, garlic soup, 'peasant omelette' with onions, potatoes and bacon, and Styrian salad with the famous pumpkin-seed oil dressing.

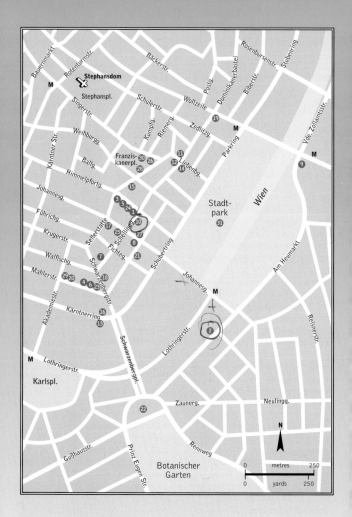

Schubertring

At the centre of this area is the Stadtpark, laid out at the same time as the Ring, the boulevard which encircles the old inner city. Many of the leading hotel restaurants are here, while the side streets are host to some historic *Beisln* and cafés.

SCHUBERTRING
Restaurants

Bacaro Rosso ❶

Schellingg. 6

☎ 513 9107

🚇 U-Bahn Stadtpark

Open: Mon–Fri 1130–2400,
Sat 1800–2400

Reservations recommended

All credit cards accepted

Italian

€€

A homely trattoria with
a rustic ambience and
engaging staff. The
excellent Italian cooking
has a Venetian bent.
Homemade pasta is
served *al dente* and the
fish dishes in particular
can be recommended.
Antipasti buffet,
Austrian and Italian
wines, coffee from
Trieste.

Dubrovnik ❷

Am Heumarkt 5

☎ 713 7102

🚇 U-Bahn Stadtpark

Open: daily 1000–2400

Reservations recommended

All credit cards accepted

Croatian

€€

You'll find this Croatian
restaurant across the
road from the Stadtpark.
The cooking has an
authentic Mediterranean
flavour though it's the
meat rather than the
fish dishes that most
appeal. Some find the
décor a bit on the

gloomy side, too sug-
gestive, perhaps, of the
long-vanished world of
Agatha Christie's novels,
a trait accentuated by
the live piano accompa-
niment at dinner.

East to West ❸

Seilerstätte 14

☎ 512 9149

🚇 U-Bahn Stubentor

Open: daily 1130–1430,
1730–2300

Reservations recommended

All credit cards accepted

International

€€

Once upon a time this
bright, cheerful eatery,
opposite the British
bookshop, was just
another Chinese restau-
rant. The current
owners have thrown
caution (and tradition)
to the wind and offer
chicken and chips,
Schnitzels, Thai and
Japanese specialities

and excellent wok dishes (very nouvelle cuisine). Try 'Inner harmony of the Samurai'.

Garibaldi Ristorante

Mahlerstr. 9

✆ 513 2165

Ⓤ U-Bahn Karlsplatz

Open: daily 1100–2400

Reservations recommended

All credit cards accepted

Italian

ⒼⒼ

The chef here makes a good stab at offering the best of Italian regional cooking. Ignore the *antipasto misto* in favour of the soup (*stracciatella alla Romana*), then order a salad to go with one of the pasta dishes. As a main course, you could choose between monk-fish (*coda di rospo alla Livornese*), grilled turbot and salmon cooked in the famous Tuscan sweet wine, Vin Santo.

Himmelpforte ⑤

Himmelpfortg. 24

✆ 513 6413

Ⓤ U-Bahn Stadtpark

Open: daily 1100–2400

Reservations recommended

All credit cards accepted

Viennese-International

ⒼⒼ

This bar-restaurant is next to the Altes Stadttheater. The mixed salads are served with Styrian pumpkin-seed oil dressing, otherwise it's the traditional Viennese cooking that makes waves – roast beef, medallions of pork stuffed with spinach and garlic cream and large helpings of roast potatoes. Loosen your belt before dessert: curd dumplings with nougat and strawberry sauce, pancakes with chocolate and nuts, ice cream … the kind of meal that used to be referred to as 'suicide with a knife and fork'!

Kervansaray ⑥

Mahlerstr. 9

✆ 512 8843

Ⓤ U-Bahn Staatsoper

Open: Mon–Sat 1200–2400

Reservations recommended

All credit cards accepted

Turkish-International

ⒼⒼⒼ

Ibrahim Dogudan's Turkish restaurant is currently rated one of the best in the city. It's hard to fault anything here: the food, especially the fish dishes, is a treat and excellent value for money, the ambience cool and refined, the service attentive, the wine selection informed and trustworthy. Lobster is the house speciality. Group menus and salad buffet.

Michl's Churrascaria ⑦

Schellingg. 12

✆ 512 0445

Ⓤ U-Bahn Karlsplatz

Open: Sun–Thu 1800–2400, Fri–Sat 1800–0100

Reservations recommended

All credit cards accepted

Brazilian

ⒼⒼ

In-your-face South American grill house where the speciality is Brazilian spit-roasts and banana fritters. The philosophy is simple: pay once and eat as much as you can from the salad bar and 12 meat dishes. There's another branch at Nussdorf (*see page 82*).

▲ Wiener Schnitzel

Pepito

Hegelg. 8

✆ 513 1345

Ⓜ U-Bahn Stadtpark

Open: daily 1800–0100
(until 0200 Fri–Sat)

Reservations recommended

All credit cards accepted

Mexican

€ €

At Pepito you can enjoy a night out on the town and still arrive in time to eat – the kitchen closes at 0100. The cooking is essentially Tex-Mex with T-bone steaks outstanding among the burritos, tacos, spicy chicken wings, and so on. Cocktails and Mexican beers available, with live music from time to time. If it's full upstairs, try the cellar.

Prinz Eugen ⑨

Hotel Hilton, Am Stadtpark 1

✆ 717 00355

Ⓜ U-Bahn Stadtpark

Open: Mon–Fri 1900–2330

Reservations recommended

All credit cards accepted

International

€ € €

Chef Marcel Vanic has established a reputation as an adventurous and capable master of the culinary arts. A pity then that the restaurant, while comfortable, is totally lacking in atmosphere. The service, however, is excellent and there's a good wine cellar. Vanic is also responsible for the Asiatic lemon grass specialities and highly creditable seafood dishes in Sam's bar and restaurant in the more upbeat, palm-decorated basement. Three-, four- and five-course set menus and children's portions available.

Puklpreiner ⑩

Schelling. 5

✆ 513 5644

Ⓜ U-Bahn Stadtpark

Open: Mon–Fri 1100–2400,
Sat 1700–2400

Reservations unnecessary

No credit cards accepted

Viennese

€ €

This friendly neighbourhood *Beisl* is next door to the Ronacher Theatre. The *Hausmannskost* is well up to standard: crisp and succulent Wiener Schnitzel, spicy beef goulash and veal liver with rice are just some of the highlights, while no one should miss out on the wild potato salad. Some outdoor seating.

SCHUBERTRING
Bars, cafés and pubs

Asahi Sushi ⑪

Stubenbastei 12

✆ 512 6561

Ⓤ U-Bahn Stephansplatz or Stubentor

Open: Mon–Sat 1130–2330, Sun 1700–2330

€€

Airy Japanese sushi bar, with grey marble floor and white wood tables. Takeaway *bento* lunches, and *sashimi* and *maki* specialities.

Bastei-Beisl ⑫

Stubenbastei 10

✆ 512 4319

Ⓤ U-Bahn Stephansplatz or Stubentor

Open: Mon–Fri 0900–2400, Sat 1100–1500, 1800–2400

€€

This useful lunch stop is only a few minutes' walk from the Stephansdom. It's not great on atmosphere, but the food is more than acceptable if you're content with a fairly predictable mix of Austrian dishes, mainly grills and fries.

Café Imperial ⑬

Hotel Imperial, Kärntner Ring 16

✆ 501 100

Ⓤ U-Bahn Karlsplatz

Open: daily 0700–2330

€€

Surprisingly few tourists discover this engaging relic of Imperial Vienna, both rooms similarly adorned with lustres, heavy brocades, tinted mirrors and gilded wallpaper. Soak in the nostalgia while sipping one of the coffee specialities, for example, *Kaisermelange* (egg yolk, honey and whipped cream).

Café Joe Albert ⑭

An der Hülben/corner of Liebenbergg.

✆ 512 2168

Ⓤ U-Bahn Stubentor

Open: Mon–Fri 0700–0100, Sun 1500–0100

€

The kitchen in this informal café is open from 0700 until 1500 for Viennese, American and English breakfasts, snacks and desserts. The lunch menu is traditional and fairly basic – Wiener Schnitzel and pike-perch, among other things.

Café-Ronacher ⑮

Seilerstätte 14

✆ 512 7279

Ⓤ U-Bahn Stadtpark

Open: Mon–Fri 0730–2300

€–€€

Cheerful café with small pavement terrace and a two-course lunch menu (Mon–Fri) – soup followed by mushroom Schnitzel with rice and salad, for example.

BETTELSTUDENT

Café Schwarzenberg 🔟

Kärntner Ring 17

✆ 512 8998

🚇 U-Bahn Karlsplatz

Open: Sun–Fri 0700–2400,
Sat 0900–2400

€

This splendid café dates
from 1861 and is the
oldest on the Ring
boulevard. To see and
be seen, find a table on
the pavement and mix
with Vienna's finest – in
the evenings often
patrons of the
Musikverein and
Konzerthaus. There's a
choice of international
newspapers which you
can pore over as you
tuck in to your Wiener
Schnitzel or *Mohr im
Hemd*. The house coffee
speciality is
Kaisermelange. The
sumptuous interior was
completely renovated
with loving attention to
detail in the late 1970s.

▲ Café Schwarzenberg

Extrablatt 🔽

Johannesg. 14

✆ 512 9834

🚇 U-Bahn Stadtpark

Open: Sun–Wed 1800–0500,
Thu–Sat 1800–0600

€€

Modern café-bar
specialising in cocktails
and appealing to a
predominantly young
clientele.

Flanagan's Irish Pub 🔘

Schwarzenbergstr. 1–3

✆ 513 7378

🚇 U-Bahn Stadtpark

Open: Sun–Thu 1300–0200,
Fri–Sat 1000–0400

€-€€

The furniture at least is
authentic, having been
removed from a pub in
Cork. Guinness and
other beers on draught
and an extensive menu
that includes fish and
chips, burger with fries,
hot mozzarella with
pesto, toasties, and, of
course, Irish stew.

Frigo 🔟

Dr-Karl-Lueger-Pl. 2

✆ 513 2145

🚇 U-Bahn Stubentor

Open: daily 1000–2300

€

Twenty-eight flavours
of organic ice cream are
on sale here and the
house speciality is
Mohneis (poppy-seed ice
cream).

El Gusto 🔟

Mahlerstr. 7

✆ 512 0673

🚇 U-Bahn Karlsplatz

Open: Mon–Fri 1500–0100,
Sat 1700–0100

€€

Attractive Spanish
bodega, serving *tapas*
and national wines. The

▲ Zum Bettelstudent

walls are lined with colourful *azulejos* (painted tiles).

Harley-Pub Milwaukee 21

Hegelg. 5

✆ 512 0513

🚇 U-Bahn Stadtpark

Open: Mon–Fri 1000–2200, Sat–Sun 1700–2200

€

You're unlikely to find many authentic bikers in this smart-looking café, serving snacks and Faschler beer.

Naschmarkt 22

Schwarzenbergpl. 16

✆ 505 3115

🚇 U-Bahn Karlsplatz

Open: Mon–Fri 1030–1930, Sat 1030–1700, Sun 1030–1500

€

Self-service restaurant offering tasty meals at bargain basement prices, including three-course daily specials.

Die Spedition 23

Mahlerstr. 13

✆ 512 8961

🚇 U-Bahn Karlsplatz

Open: Mon–Thu 0800–2100, Fri 0800–1700

€

Gemütlich (cosy) just about sums up this traditional wood-panelled café. There's a vegetarian menu as well as the usual range of meat dishes (chicken liver and pork ragout, for example); breakfast is also available.

Zum Altes Stadttheater 24

Himmelpfortg. 24

✆ 512 5302

🚇 U-Bahn Stadtpark

Open: Mon–Fri 0630–0100

€–**€€**

The architectural splendours of the Ronacher variety theatre can be admired from the café opposite. The menu is traditional *Hausmannskost* – such as beef with apple sauce or calves' liver with roast potatoes, though there's usually a vegetarian speciality or two.

Zum Bettelstudent 25

Johannesg. 12

✆ 513 2044

🚇 U-Bahn Stadtpark

Open: Sun–Thu 1000–0200, Fri–Sat 1000–0300

€€

'The Hard up Student' is a large rambling pub, spread over two floors. At weekends in particular it's a popular meeting place for young people of all kinds, and after about 2200 it's standing room only. Food (all reasonably priced) is served throughout the day – the choice includes spare ribs, pizza, steaks, filled rolls and hot 'n' spicy chilli con carne.

Zu den Drei Hacken 26

Singerstr. 28

✆ 512 5895

🚇 U-Bahn Stubentor

Open: Mon–Sat 0900–2400

€€

Franz Schubert was a regular patron of this quaint little *Beisl*, still frequented by local office workers and students as well as tourists. The cuisine is pretty eclectic – everything from *Salzburger Nockerl* to liver dumpling soup and tortellini. In summer look for a table in the peaceful and surprisingly spacious *Gastgarten*.

SCHUBERTRING
Shops, markets and picnic sites

Johann Wolfbauer 27

Johannesg. 23

Ⓤ U-Bahn Stadtpark

Open: Mon–Fri 0630–1800, Sat 0630–1200

August bakery and confectioner's dating from the time of the Habsburgs (1853). Apart from the various breads, cakes and brioches, there's a robust ham and egg breakfast or single-course lunch.

Grocers and supermarkets

Isabella 28

Seilerstätte 27

Ⓤ U-Bahn Stubentor

Open: Mon–Fri 0700–1900, Sat 0700–1200

Small bakery and grocer's shop.

Nespresso 29

Mahlerstr. 7

Ⓤ U-Bahn Karlsplatz

Open: Mon–Fri 0900–1900, Sat 0930–1700

There's more to an espresso than meets the eye, as you'll discover when you visit this intriguing coffee shop. Let the assistants take you through the options – *ristretto*, *arpeggio, capriccio, volluto, Livanto* … Sample the different strengths and blends of Arabian, South American and African beans before you decide.

Wines

Grams & Co 30

Singerstrasse 26

Ⓤ U-Bahn Stubentor

Open: Mon–Fri 0900–1800, Sat 0900–1300

This prominent wine merchant's, just a couple of minutes' walk from the Stephansdom, occupies the 700-year-old cellar of a medieval convent. Beaujolais and French champagnes, grappa, Kirsch, apricot and cherry brandy liqueurs, Madeira and port can all be specially gift-wrapped to make the ideal birthday or Christmas present.

Picnic sites

Stadtpark 31

Ⓤ U-Bahn Stadtpark

This charming landscaped park was laid out by Rudolf Siebeck and Josef Selleny in 1857–62 with shady paths, ornamental ponds, playful waterfalls and statues commemorating famous artists and composers. Aesthetically, it forms part of the ambitious Ringstrasse development which replaced the fortifications built to withstand Turkish attack in the 17th century. The neo-Rennaisance **Kursalon** is now Vienna's premier casino. During the 1860s the waltz-king, Johann Strauss, and his orchestra gave concerts here to please the cream of Austrian society.

▲ Stadtpark

Hotel restaurants

Up-market dining

Some of Vienna's top chefs work in the city's leading hotels. While the price of dinner can be prohibitive, you can often eat more cheaply at lunchtime or in the less formal surroundings of the second-string eatery.

• **Altwienerhof** *Herklotzg. 6; ✆ 892 6000;* Ⓜ *U-Bahn Gumpendorferstrasse; open: daily 1100–1100; reservations recommended; all credit cards accepted; French-International;* ❶❷❸. Seasoned diners make regular pilgrimages to this gourmet temple, despite its location in a run-down part of the city. The Altwienerhof has been in the hands of the Kellner family from its opening in 1928. The flawless cooking has a pronounced French accent, Rudi Kellner's personal homage to the Escoffier tradition. The wine cellar (of 23,000 bottles) is one of the finest in Europe and includes some wonderful old Burgundies. French tapestries add a touch of class to the dining rooms but maybe a little too much formality. You may prefer to reserve a table in the charming winter garden and conservatory. Business lunches and set menus of up to eight courses available.

• **Anna Sacher** *Hotel Sacher, Philharmonikerstr. 4; ✆ 514 56-0;* Ⓜ *U-Bahn Karlsplatz; open: daily 1130–1500, 1800– 2330; reservations recommended; all credit cards accepted; Viennese-International;* ❶❷❸. Anna Sacher ran the hotel for nearly 40 years until 1930 and was famous for her love of cigars. The food here is of the highest standard, but the ambience can be a little formal – many guests prefer to eat in the more relaxed surroundings of the **Red Bar**.

• **Le Ciel** *ANA Grand Hotel Wien, Kärntner Ring 9; ✆ 515 809100;* Ⓜ *U-Bahn Karlsplatz; open: Mon–Sat 1200–1430, 1900– 2245; reservations recommended; all credit cards accepted; Viennese-French;* ❶❷❸. Le Ciel is fast making a name for itself as one of the best restaurants for classic Viennese and French cuisine. There's an affordable business menu at lunchtimes and three-, four- and five-course set menus in the evening. Or you can take a chance on the personal selections of chef Siegfried Pucher. The cheese trolley deserves a special

▲ König von Ungarn

mention. Live piano music 2000 to 2400.

• **Hotel im Palais Schwarzenberg** *Schwarzenbergpl. 9; ✆ 798 4515;* 🚇 *U-Bahn Karlsplatz; open: daily 1200–1430, 1800–2300; reservations essential; all credit cards accepted; Viennese-French;* ❶❶❶. The Schwarzenberg Palace was designed in 1720 by the great Austrian architect Fischer von Erlach. The restaurant comprises two dining spaces – the elegant **Roter Salon** and the glass-fronted terrace with fabulous views of the park. While the cooking has panache, some dishes are spoilt by over-elaboration. Overall, the hors-d'oeuvres and fish dishes come off best.

• **Imperial** *Hotel Imperial, Kärntner Ring 16; ✆ 501 100;* 🚇 *U-Bahn Karlsplatz; open: daily 1800–2400; reservations recommended; all credit cards accepted; Austrian-International;* ❶❶❶. The Imperial wins high marks for the adventurousness of its 'New Viennese Cuisine', given a Styrian twist here by head chef Stefan Hierzer. The service is impeccable while the lustres, wood-panelled surrounds and dynastic portraits hark back to a nobler age. Recommended: prime Styrian beef served with *Krautfleckerln* (pasta squares stuffed with cabbage and onions) and a pumpkin-seed oil dressing.

• **König von Ungarn** *Schulerstr. 10; ✆ 512 5319;* 🚇 *U-Bahn Stephansplatz; open: Sun–Fri*

1145–1430, 1800–2230; reservations recommended; all credit cards accepted; International; ❶❶❶. Within sight of the Stephansdom, the 'King of Hungary' café-restaurant is located in the splendid courtyard of an historic hotel, founded in the same year as the Congress of Vienna (1815). Diners can choose from half a dozen set menus which feature beef (the house speciality), grilled catfish, poached salmon, saddle of milk lamb in thyme and veal chops. However, it's the hors-d'oeuvres and the desserts that really shine here.

• **Vier Jahreszeiten** *Inter-Continental Wien, Johannesg. 28; ✆ 711220;* 🚇 *U-Bahn Stadtpark; open: restaurant Mon–Fri 1100–1500, 1800–2300; brasserie daily 0630–2400; reservations recommended; all credit cards accepted; International;* ❶❶–❶❶❶. The kitchen at the 'Four Seasons' is presided over by master chef, Manfred Buchinger, renowned for his light touch and creative flair. Crustaceans are his speciality but the menu (changing with the seasons) is wide-ranging and international in spirit. While there can be few complaints about the food, the dining room lacks atmosphere, a failing accentuated by the languid improvisations of the pianist. There's a breakfast and lunchtime buffet and a choice of set menus at dinner if you don't wish to dine à la carte. You can eat almost as well and more cheaply in the **Brasserie Am Stadtpark**.

> ... grilled catfish, poached salmon, saddle of milk lamb in thyme and veal chops ...

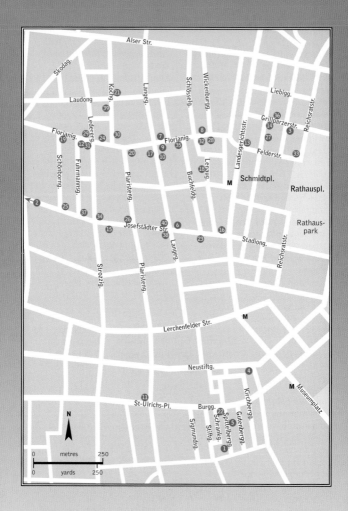

Josefstadt

This residential area, to the west of the Old City, was laid out in the 18th century on the orders of Josef II. The large student population has created a demand for cheap bars and restaurants of all kinds, mainly around Florianigasse.

JOSEFSTADT
Restaurants

Boheme ❶

Spittelbergg. 19

✆ 523 3173

🚇 U-Bahn Volkstheater

Open: Mon–Sat 1800–2400

Reservations recommended

All credit cards accepted

Viennese

💰💰

Diners who visit this engaging wine tavern are treated to recorded selections from classical opera as they sample the reasonably successful Viennese dishes. Good choice of Austrian wines and some outside seating during the summer.

Die fromme Helene ❷

Josefstädterstr. 91

✆ 406 9144

🚇 Tram J

Open: Mon–Fri 1130–1430, 1800–2400, Sat 1800–2400

Reservations unnecessary

All credit cards accepted

Viennese

💰💰

An appealing little restaurant with a warm atmosphere and old-fashioned décor. The Viennese cuisine is usually up to the mark and the service is excellent.

Fish and Orange ❸

Ebendorferstr. 10

✆ 408 7071

🚇 U-Bahn Rathaus

Open: Mon–Fri 0900–0100, Sat 1800–0100

Reservations recommended

All credit cards accepted

Fish

💰💰

The striking blue-and-orange décor of this fish restaurant makes an instant impact. The cooking too wins high marks, but the large unbroken dining space only works when the place is busy. River and sea fish, including pike, devil fish and salmon, plus an extensive wine list.

Karrer ❹

Neustiftg. 5

✆ 526 9448

🚇 U-Bahn Volkstheater

▲ Spittelberg

Open: Mon–Fri 1130–1500, 1800–2330

Reservations recommended

All credit cards accepted

Viennese

A small, elegant restaurant, popular with actors and patrons of the Volkstheater. The young team now in charge strives to please while the Viennese dishes are prepared with an uncommonly light and creative touch.

Kochwerkstatt ⑤

Spittelbergg. 8

☎ 523 3291

🚇 U-Bahn Volkstheater

Open: Tue–Sun 1900–2400

Reservations unnecessary

No credit cards accepted

Viennese

€€

A typical neighbourhood *Lokal*, Kochwerkstatt wins friends with its easygoing, no-nonsense approach to dining out. Oliver the chef likes to do his own thing in the kitchen with interesting, broadly favourable results.

Levante ⑥

Josefstädterstr. 14

☎ 408 5306

🚇 Tram J

Open: daily 1130–2330

Reservations unnecessary

All credit cards accepted

Turkish

€€

This friendly Turkish restaurant (one of a

chain) serves up delicious *mezes* (starters) as well as the usual kebab specialities. The pitta bread, baked in a wood-fired oven, is a real treat.

Lima ⑦

Florianig. 16

☎ 403 1815

🚇 U-Bahn Rathaus

Open: Mon–Sat 1700–4000

Reservations recommended

South American

€€

This cheerful cantina offers a combination of Peruvian and Argentinian specialities, including *ceviche* (raw fish marinated in lemon), *papa a la Huancaina* (potato dish) and *lomo saltado* (Argentine beef with tomato, onions, potato and rice). Also tempting is the *arroz a la cubana* – rice with fried egg and banana. There's a choice of beers and wines from Peru, Mexico and Bolivia. Leisurely service allows time to take advantage of lessons in tango and salsa, should you be so minded!

Neues Rathaus (Hermann Adam) ⑧

Florianig. 2

☎ 408 0112

🚇 U-Bahn Rathaus

Open: Mon–Fri: coffeehouse 0800–2400, restaurant 1100–2400

Reservations recommended

All credit cards accepted

Viennese

€€

An old favourite with politicians, university professors and their students, this eatery is best described as a *Wirtshaus* (inn). Most Viennese plump for the game specialities but there are also one or two simple fish dishes, fillet of pikeperch (*Zander*), for example. The cooking is nothing special but there's Stiegl beer from Salzburg by way of compensation. If you're averse to smoking you can take refuge in the pleasant courtyard.

Oliva Verde ⑨

Florianig. 15

☎ 405 4106

🚇 U-Bahn Rathaus

Open: Mon–Fri 1200–1500, 1800–2400, Sat–Sun 1800–2400

Reservations recommended

All credit cards accepted

Italian

€€

Pizzas are the mainstay of this friendly neighbourhood trattoria. They're made using spelt (wheat flour) and cooked in the traditional wood-fired oven; there are more than 20 different toppings to choose from. If you're not in the mood for pizza, there's *bruschetta*, carpaccio and a large selection of pasta alternatives. Everything on the menu is prepared using only organic ingredients. Drinks include wines and Ottakringer beer.

Schnattl 🔟

Langeg. 40

☎ 405 3400

🚇 U-Bahn Rathaus

Open: Mon–Fri 1130–1430, 1800–2400, Sat 1800–2400

Reservations recommended

💳 American Express

Viennese

💰💰

One of the more stylish eateries in Josefstadt, Schnattl's greatest asset is its wonderful garden. The cooking, like the post-modern setting, has a touch of glamour about it, and there are some unusual offerings such as medallions of mountain ram. Excellent choice of wines and at least one lunch special available.

Spatzennest 1️⃣1️⃣

St-Ulrichs-Pl. 1

☎ 526 1659

🚇 U-Bahn Volkstheater

Open: Sun–Thu 0900–2400

Reservations recommended

💰

Viennese

💰💰

The 'Sparrow's Nest' is a good choice if you're keen on trying out authentic Viennese home cooking using traditional recipes. This typical Austrian inn looks its best in the summer when guests can enjoy the view of St Ulrich's from the garden. Said to be a

haunt of politicians – a plus or a minus?

La Tavolozza 1️⃣2️⃣

Florianig. 37

☎ 406 3757

🚇 U-Bahn Rathaus

Open: Mon–Fri 1800–0100, Sat–Sun 1200–1500, 1800–0100

Reservations recommended

💳

Italian

💰💰

A cut above the average Italian restaurant, La Tavolozza gets high marks from its Viennese patrons for service, ambience and prices (very reasonable indeed). Fish is the spe-ciality but there's also a good choice of pizzas.

▲ Spatzennest

JOSEFSTADT
Bars, cafés and pubs

Bogside Inn 13

Landesgerichtsstr. 18

✆ 409 6490

🚇 U-Bahn Rathaus

Open: Mon–Fri 1100–0200,
Sat–Sun 1700–0200

●–●●

As the name none too subtly suggests, Bogside is an Irish pub with the usual virtues – Kilkenny and Caffreys on tap and cheapish eats including Galway shepherd's pie, Irish stew, fish and chips and sandwiches.

Büro 14

Rathausstr. 11

✆ 405 0677

🚇 U-Bahn Rathaus

Open: Mon–Fri 1000–0200,
Sat 1800–0200

●●

Friendly unpretentious café-bar offering a range of Viennese and Italian dishes. DJ at weekends.

Café Coural 15

Josefstädterstr. 35

✆ 405 2406

🚇 Tram J

Open: Mon–Sat 0800–2300

●●

Busy *Lokal* offering a good choice of breakfasts and an extensive vegetarian menu – unusual in Vienna. Regulars sit around the bar drinking Puntigammer beer on draught.

Café Eiles 16

Josefstädterstr. 2

✆ 405 3410

🚇 Tram J

Open: daily 0700–2200

●●

On the corner of Lenaugasse, this long-established café (1901) is now showing signs of wear and tear. Somehow this only adds to the appeal. The locals come here to read the newspapers and for a bit of peace and quiet – the Sachertorte too is worth investigating.

Café Roschmann 17

Langeg. 35

✆ 406 4393

U-Bahn Rathaus

Open: Mon–Fri 0630–2000,
Sat 0700–1200

€

A dark, smoky bar near
the Rathaus (town hall),
serving breakfasts and
light meals including
homemade desserts.

Centimeter I

Lenaug. 11

✆ 405 7808

 U-Bahn Rathaus

Open: Mon–Fri 1000–0200,
Sat 1100–0200, Sun 1100–
2400

€–€€

Popular with tourists
and locals, this large,
busy pub is strong on
draught and bottled
beers – Stiegl,
Budweiser, Hirter,
Zwickl and Löwenbräu
to name but a few. The
enthusiasm for pub
culture here is infectious
so you may be tempted
to stay for a light lunch
or evening meal: egg
dumplings with salad,
pancakes and fresh
bread, sold by the
centimetre.

Florianhof 19

Florianig. 45

✆ 402 4842

 U-Bahn Rathaus

Open: Mon–Fri 0800–0200,
Sat–Sun 1000–0200

€–€€

An excellent
coffeehouse serving
reasonably priced, high-
quality light meals of
the goulash variety.
Breakfasts include
waffles, cornflakes, fresh
orange juice and toast,

and you can catch up
on the Austrian and
international press as
you tuck in.

Gasthaus Hummer 20

Florianig. 19

✆ 408 3038

 U-Bahn Rathaus

Open: Mon–Fri 1100–1400,
1800–2230

€€

Hale and hearty *Beisl*,
serving homely
Viennese dishes such as
Wiener Schnitzel (pork
not veal), goulash and
meat platter 'peasant
style'.

Japan Grillhaus 21

Laudong. 24

✆ 405 7188

 U-Bahn Rathaus

Open: daily 1130–1430,
1800–2300

€€

As much sushi as you
can eat. The house spe-
cialities are *shabu shabu*
(Japanese stew-pot) and

rolled duck cooked in a
special sauce.

Lux 22

Schrankg. 4/Spittelbergg. 3

✆ 526 9491

 U-Bahn Volkstheater

Open: daily 1000–0200

€

The jury is still out on
the culinary
accomplishments of this
self-styled 'alternative
coffeehouse'. The
vegetarian dishes make
a welcome change from
the usual meat diet and
the lovely glass-covered
terrace is the other big
plus – members of
Austria's Green Party
meet constituents here.

Marienhof 23

Josefstädterstr. 9

✆ 408 8905

 Tram J

Open: Mon–Fri 1100–2400,
Sat–Sun 1730–0100

€€

Friendly, rather smoky
Beisl with a garden

open until 2200. The food is standard Viennese fare – try the baked calves' liver with potato salad or the homemade sausages.

Merkur

Floriang. 18

✆ 405 0487

Ⓤ U-Bahn Rathaus

Open: daily 0900–0200

€

This cheap and cheerful *Beisl* is very 'in' with students and young people. The menu is eclectic to say the least – everything from pancakes to moussaka. The studiedly down-at-heel ambience is the other source of Merkur's appeal.

Ruffino ㉕

Josefstädterstr. 48

✆ 406 4540

Ⓣ Tram J

Open: daily 1100–2400

€–€€

Bustling at lunchtime, Ruffino's is a pizzeria which also turns its hand to standard Italian dishes such as *scallopina alla Milanese* and seafood risotto. Wines include Lambrusco, Frascati and Bardollino, served by the glass or bottle.

Samuri ㉖

Josefstädterstr. 20

✆ 409 4551

Ⓣ Tram J

Open: Mon–Sat 1130–2300

€

Small high-street sushi bar specialising in *maki*

dishes. Start with the *miso* soup.

San Giovanni ㉗

Rathausstr. 11

✆ 407 4235

Ⓤ U-Bahn Rathaus

Open: Mon–Fri 1100–1430, 1730–2300, Sun 1700–2300

€–€€

The salads here almost outshine the pizzas – try the San Giovanni special with an order of fresh mussels. Most of the other dishes seem to come with broccoli!

Scarabocchio ㉘

Floriang. 3

✆ 405 2727

Ⓤ U-Bahn Rathaus

Open: Mon–Fri 1130–1430, 1700–2300, Sat–Sun 1730–2330

€€

Tasty pizzas cooked in a wood-fired oven are nicely complemented by appetising salads – *rucola* with parmesan, for example. The hot *antipasti* include a delicious *pappadelle al forno*, while the main courses feature fish as well as the predictable lamb, veal and chicken specialities.

Ti Amo ㉙

Floriang. 34

✆ 0676 470 8151

Ⓤ U-Bahn Rathaus

Open: daily 1800–0200

€€

A cross between an Italian *osteria* and a Viennese *Beisl*, this tiny wine bar also serves

Krombach and Murau beers on draught as well as an appetising range of snacks including *crostini*.

Toscana ㉚

Kochg. 4

✆ 408 1879

Ⓣ Tram J

Open: daily 1130–1430, 1700–2330

€–€€

It's difficult to find anything specifically Tuscan here; all the same, the pizzas and other Italian dishes, including *saltimbocca alla Romana*, pass muster. The modern no-frills ambience attracts a youthful clientele.

Vierhundert Beisl ㉛

Floriang. 35

✆ 408 1174

Ⓤ U-Bahn Rathaus

Open: daily 1800–0100

€€

Old Viennese specialities (spicy beef, steak and onions, Schnitzel, herring salad) are served in this 19th-century hostelry with the traditional wood and glass partitions intact.

Zur Wickenburg ㉜

Floriang. 3

✆ 408 1780

Ⓤ U-Bahn Rathaus

Open: Mon–Fri 0700–2400

€–€€

Café-bar specialising in Hungarian soups, goulash and sausages. Ham and eggs available for breakfasts.

JOSEFSTADT
Shops, markets and picnic sites

Bakeries

Konditorei Sluka 33

Rathauspl. 8

🚇 U-Bahn Rathaus

Open: Mon–Fri 0800–1900,
Sat 0800–1730

Located in a smart
arcade on Rathausplatz,
this well-known
Konditorei sells half a
dozen different varieties
of strudels as well as
roulades and desserts.
There's also an appetis-
ing buffet. Tables are set
out under the arcade.

Mailler & Tichy 34

Josefstädterstr. 34

🚋 Tram J

Open: Mon–Fri 0600–1900,
Sat 0700–1700, Sun 0800–
1200

Large baker's shop sell-
ing the usual range of
Austrian breads, filled
rolls and pastries.

Grocers and supermarkets

Emma 35

Florianig. 9

🚇 U-Bahn Rathaus

Open: Mon–Fri 0730–1900,
Sat 0730–1600

Supermarket with small
deli counter where you
can buy sandwiches and
other snacks.

Feinkost zur Rathaus Klimon 36

Grillparzerstr. 2

🚇 U-Bahn Rathaus

Open: Mon–Fri 0630–1800

This grocery store near
the Rathaus has an
enticing delicatessen
counter. You can also
buy wines and the
famous Florentine
almond biscuits, *cantuc-
cini alla mandorla*.

Fein und Köstlich 37

Josefstädterstr./corner of
Fuhrmannsg.

🚋 Tram J

Open: Mon–Fri 0700–1900,
Sat 0730–1700

Small delicatessen offer-
ing a dish of the day, as
well as salads, burgers
and other snacks.

Kräuter Reformshaus 38

Josefstädterstr. 19

🚋 Tram J

Open: Mon–Fri 0830–1900,
Sat 0900–1700

An Aladdin's cave sell-
ing everything from
couscous and salads to
fruit juices, Austrian
wines, nuts, dried fruit
and organic and low-fat
health foods.

Mezze 39

Kochg. 13

🚌 Bus 13A

Open: Mon–Fri 0700–2000,
Sat 0730–1300

Turkish and Greek
delicacies including
cheeses, olives, bottles
of *retsina* and *raki*. The
delicatessen counter
sells *dolmas*, salads and
a delicious spinach
strudel.

Zielpunkt 40

Josefstädterstr. 18

🚋 Tram J

Open: Mon–Fri 0730–1830,
0730–1800

You'll find this branch
of the well-known
Austrian supermarket
chain on the corner of
Langegasse.

The best of the rest

Venturing further afield

Vienna is so well blessed with restaurants that it's impossible to cover them all. The following selection includes some of the better-known suburban eateries and a few central ones that would otherwise have escaped the net.

• **Altes Bürgermeisterhaus** *Cobenzlg. 40; ∅ 320 7223;* 🔊 *bus 38A; open: daily 1130–2400; reservations unnecessary; all credit cards accepted; Viennese;* ❸❸❸. An authentic *Heurige*, furnished in the Biedermeier style favoured by the 19th-century Austrian bourgeoisie. Feast on classic Viennese dishes such as *Tafelspitz* while being entertained by traditional gypsy music. Large garden.

• **Bamkraxler** *Kahlenbergerstr. 17; ∅ 318 8800;* 🔊 *U-Bahn Nussdorf, then taxi; open: Thu–Sat 1600–2400, Sun 1130–2400; reservations recommended; no credit cards accepted; Viennese;* ❸❸. The big plus at this *Heurige* is the lovely garden, with chestnut trees for shade and a playground for the kids.

▲ Donauturm restaurant

Unusually, the musical entertainment is jazz and blues rather than *Schrammel* and it's the beers rather than the wines that catch the eye.

• **Cobenzl** *Am Cobenzl 94; ∅ 320 5120;* 🔊 *bus 38A; open: restaurant Mon–Sat 1830–2400, Sun 1130–1800; café daily 1100–2200; reservations essential; all credit cards accepted; Viennese;* ❸❸–❸❸❸. Famous for its views, Schloss Cobenzl was once a monastic headquarters of the Jesuits. Famous guests of the restaurant have included US President John F Kennedy, Queen Elizabeth II and Elton John. Both the café and restaurant enjoy panoramic views of Vienna.

• **Do & Co** *Haas Haus, Stephanspl. 12; ∅ 535 3969;* 🔊 *U-Bahn Stephansplatz; open: daily 1200–1500, 1800–2400; reservations essential; all credit cards accepted; Austrian-International;* ❸❸❸. Although the menu features Austrian and Mediterranean dishes, the cuisine at this restaurant in the shadow of the Stephansdom is best described as eclectic – American steaks, sushi, Thai soups and stir-fries. The cooking is undistinguished but most of the guests are too busy admiring the view to care.

• **Donauturm** *Donauturmstr. 4; ∅ 263 3573;* 🔊 *U-Bahn Alte Donau; open: daily 1000–2400;*

reservations recommended; all credit cards accepted; International; ❶❶–❶❶❶. The sky-puncturing communications tower, in a park next to the UNO City complex, has two eateries – a café at 160m and a restaurant at 170m. On a good day the views are phenomenal, as far as Hungary to the south and towards the Wachau in the west. As for the food, it's mainly roast dishes.

> **On a good day the views are phenomenal, as far as Hungary to the south and towards the Wachau in the west.**

• **Grünauer** *Hermanng. 32;* ✆ *526 4080;* Ⓜ *tram 49; open: Mon 1800–2400, Tue–Fri 1130–1500, 1800–2400; reservations essential; no credit cards accepted; Viennese;* ❶❶. This small, out-of-town *Beisl* serves some of the finest *Hausmannskost* (home cooking) in Austria. It's also becoming something of a mecca for wine enthusiasts. The menu changes on a daily basis but never disappoints. The ambience is relaxed and unpretentious.

• **Melker Stiftskeller** *Schotteng. 3;* ✆ *533 5530;* Ⓜ *U-Bahn Schottentor; open: Tue–Sat 1700–2400; Austrian;* ❶❶. Located in an atmospheric monastic cellar, the *Wachauer* wines come from the great Austrian abbey of Melk (ask for Jochinger Riesling). The house speciality is *Stelze* (shin of pork with bread dumplings, cabbage salad and horseradish).

• **Oswald & Kalb** *Bäckerstr. 14;* ✆ *512 1371;* Ⓜ *U-Bahn Stephansplatz; open: daily 1800–0200; reservations essential; all credit cards accepted; Austrian;*

❶–❶❶❶. Up-market *Beisl* with a handsome wooden façade and a menu that changes every day but which focuses on Viennese and Styrian dishes. The cooking is classy enough to put it in the gourmet league but word gets round fast – if you arrive without reserving a table, you haven't a prayer.

• **Schöll** *Cobenzlg. 108;* ✆ *320 6907;* Ⓜ *bus 38A; open: daily 1600–2400; reservations unnecessary; no credit cards accepted; Viennese;* ❶❶. Traditional *Buschenschank* (wine tavern) offering an authentic rustic setting. Great atmosphere and excellent value for money – especially the cold buffet.

• **A Tavola** *Weihburgg. 3–5;* ✆ *512 7955;* Ⓜ *U-Bahn Stephansplatz; open: Mon–Sat 1130–1430, 1800–2300; reservations essential; all credit cards accepted; Italian;* ❶❶. From the same stable as the Cantinetta Antinori, this suave Tuscan outfit offers regional Italian cooking of equal sophistication and refinement.

• **Zum Posthorn** *Posthorng. 6;* ✆ *713 344;* Ⓜ *U-Bahn Rochusgasse; open: Mon–Fri 1800–2400; reservations recommended; no credit cards accepted; Austrian;* ❶❶. Sociable *Beisl* with Carinthian and Slovenian specialities as well as traditional Viennese cooking at bargain prices. Choice of Austrian or Italian wines, with dark or light Hirter lager on draught if you prefer.

Grinzing

Vienna still barely encroaches on this lovely 'suburban village', famous for the vineyard inns known as *Heurige*.

GRINZING
Restaurants

Alter Klosterkeller im Passauer-hof ❶

Cobenzlg. 9

✆ 0222 32 6345

🚌 Bus 38A

Open: daily 1600–2400

Reservations unnecessary

All credit cards accepted

Viennese

€€

The 12th-century Romanesque foundations of a monastic wine cellar have been incorporated into this handsome *Heurige*, a roomy place with two gardens.

The hot and cold buffet is nothing special.

Altes Presshaus ❷

Cobenzlg. 15

✆ 320 0203

🚌 Bus 38A

Open: Mar–Dec daily 1600–2400

Reservations unnecessary

All credit cards accepted

Viennese

€€€

The Old Presshaus claims to have the oldest wine cellar in Grinzing, dating from 1527. There's a hot and

cold buffet, or you can dine à la carte if you prefer. One caveat: the huge garden makes this *Heurige* a likely target for tour parties. Live *Schrammelmusik* every evening.

Bach-Hengl ❸

Sandg. 7–9

✆ 320 2439

🚌 Bus 38A

Open: daily 1600–2400

Reservations unnecessary

All credit cards accepted

Viennese

€€

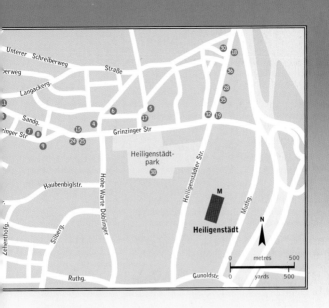

▲ *Schrammelmusik* players

One of the largest *Heurige* in Grinzing (the garden can accommodate 1000 people), Bach-Hengl is a charming inn with old statues, lamps and other bric-à-brac in the courtyard and a tradition of viticulture spanning nine centuries. While the hot and cold buffet is nothing to write home about, the *gemischter Satz* is excellent and there's *Schrammelmusik* on fiddle and accordion for good measure. Children's play area in the garden.

Brummbärli

Armbrusterg. 9	
✆ 318 9846	
🚍 Bus 38A	
Open: Tue–Fri 1100–1430, 1800–2300, Sat 1100–2300, Sun 1100–1500	
Reservations recommended	
All credit cards accepted	
Viennese	
€€€	

Named after its large collection of teddy bears, Brummbärli is a roomy *Heurige* offering a choice of draught beers as well as wines and seasonal specialities such as fried lambs' liver with sausage, tomato and rice, beef tartare with toast and butter, and pork roast. Spare ribs on Wednesdays.

Engelhardt Restaurant 'Zur schönen Aussicht' 5

Pfarrpl. 5	
✆ 318 8000	

🚍 Bus 38A	
Open: Mon, Wed–Sat 1130–2400, Sun 1100–1700	
Reservations essential	
All credit cards accepted	
Viennese	
€€€	

The beautiful view from the summer garden is what gives this restaurant its name. The dining rooms have an intimate feel and date back to the Middle Ages – the building itself is 800 years old. While the food isn't cheap, it's of a high standard and there are fixed price menus for lunch and dinner.

Familie Muth 6

Probusg. 10	
✆ 372 247	
🚍 Bus 38A	
Open: Tue–Sun 1530–2400	
Reservations recommended	
All credit cards accepted	
Viennese	
€€	

The Muth family has been involved in the wine-growing business since 1683 so it's hardly surprising that they've won prizes – witness the excellent Traminer. The speciality of the house is a fruit strudel prepared according to an old Viennese recipe. There's a shady garden with children's play area.

Feuerwehr-Wagner 7

Grinzingerstr. 53	
✆ 320 2442	
🚍 Bus 38A	

Open: daily 1600–2400	
Reservations unnecessary	
All credit cards accepted	
Viennese	
€€	

The garden setting is wonderful but you may feel the prices overly exploit this undoubted asset. *Backhendl* (chicken fried in paprika and cream) is the house speciality, while the hot and cold buffet features several vegetarian dishes.

Figlmüller's 8

Grinzingerstr. 55	
✆ 320 4257	
🚍 Bus 38A	
Open: Mon–Sat 1630–2400 (Fri–Sat only in Nov–Dec)	
Reservations recommended	
All credit cards accepted	
Viennese	
€€€	

Figlmüller's *Heurige* restaurant, in a charming Biedermeier house, has a garden with a covered glass roof to protect diners against inclement weather. It's famous for its huge Wiener Schnitzels and there are twice-daily performances of traditional Viennese songs. *See page 49 also.*

Francesco 9

Grinzingerstr. 50	
✆ 368 23 11	
🚍 Bus 38A	
Open: daily 1130–2400	
Reservations recommended	
All credit cards accepted	
Italian	
€€–€€€	

Finding an Italian restaurant in the heart of *Heurige* country is an unexpected but welcome surprise. Francesco's lies just off the main road and looks like an old coaching inn. Pizzas are the mainstay, cooked in the traditional wood-fired oven, and children's portions are available on request. Alternatively, there's a dish of the day and a rotating weekly menu of pasta, seafood and grilled meat offerings. Wines include a good Chianti Classico from the Antinori stable. The stone counter and timber décor give the place a cool, rustic feel, or you can eat al fresco in the large back garden.

Grinzingerhof

Grinzingerallee 86	
✆ 320 6483	
🚍 Bus 38A	
Open: Mon–Sat 1100–2300, Sun 0900–1700	

Reservations unnecessary	
All credit cards accepted	
Viennese	
€€	

This hotel-restaurant with a large garden specialises in robust home cooking. If you're in an adventurous frame of mind, try the *Beuschl* (lung of venison) or the incredibly filling chef's goulash (made with leg of beef, garlic, gherkins, sausages, egg and potatoes). The dumplings are made with cheese or spinach, with red pepper for extra zest. For dessert try the classic *Mohr im Hemd* (chocolate walnut cake with chocolate sauce and whipped cream).

Hans Maly

Sandg. 8	
✆ 320 1384	
🚍 Bus 38A	
Open: Mar–Oct daily 1530–2400	

Reservations unnecessary	
All credit cards accepted	
Viennese	
€€	

Wine has been a family business here since 1829, as the ceramic crest of green and red grapes indicates. The home cooking too is up to the mark and there's plenty of shade in the summer garden. *Schrammelmusik* on fiddle and accordion.

Hauermandel

Cobenzlg. 20	
✆ 320 3027	
🚍 Bus 38A	
Open: Mon–Sat 1730–2400	
Reservations recommended	
All credit cards accepted	
Viennese	
€€	

Wine has been sold on the premises of this *Heurige* since 1740. In 1805 French troops were quartered here as

Napoleon's army advanced on Vienna. The salad buffet and seasonal dishes are reasonably priced and there's a large garden where guests are treated to live performances of *Schrammelmusik*. A bit touristy for some tastes.

Hengl-Haselbrunner 13

Iglaseeg. 10	
℘ 320 3330	
🚊 Tram 38	
Open: daily 1530–2400	
Reservations recommended	
All credit cards accepted	
Viennese	
ⓖⓖ–ⓖⓖⓖ	

A traditional *Heurige* offering visitors a hot and cold buffet with outstanding desserts. However, it's the wines here, specifically the Rieslings, that have won the plaudits of Austrian food critics. Large, attractive garden.

Heurigenschank 14

Cobenzlg. 34	
℘ 320 3233	
🚌 Bus 38A	
Open: Mon–Fri 1800–2400, Sat–Sun 1130–2400	
Reservations unnecessary	
All credit cards accepted	
Viennese	
ⓖⓖ	

This classic *Heurige* has extra seating in the gallery on the first floor. The fare is solid and traditional with Schnitzels, *Gröstl* and *Tafelspitz* to the fore and Emperor dumplings

thrown in for good measure. Desserts include strudels and apricot pancakes.

Jade 15

Grinzingerstr. 71–3	
℘ 320 6896	
🚌 Bus 38A	
Open: daily 1130–1430, 1730–2330	
Reservations recommended	
All credit cards accepted	
Chinese	
ⓖⓖ	

It may seem perverse coming all the way to Grinzing for a Chinese meal, but for those who feel the call, Jade can offer garden seating as well as a taste of Shanghai. Quality food with outstanding fish and rice dishes. There's another branch at **Favoritenstrasse 177** (℘ *602 6295*).

Kirchenstöckl 16

Cobenzlg. 3	
℘ 320 6662	
🚌 Bus 38A	
Open: daily 1130–2400	
Reservations recommended	
All credit cards accepted	
Viennese	
ⓖ–ⓖⓖ	

In the Middle Ages this *Heurige* restaurant served as Grinzing's bath house. The garden here is on the small side but the food is good and there's a large choice of wines. Recommended: spare ribs, black pudding, homemade Emperor's Nonsense

(*Kaiserschmarrn*), a kind of pancake/omelette, served in this instance in a plum sauce.

Mayer am Pfarrplatz 17

Pfarrpl. 2	
℘ 370 1287	
🚌 Bus 38A	
Open: Mon–Sat 1600–2400, Sun 1100–2400	
Reservations recommended	
All credit cards accepted	
Viennese	
ⓖⓖ	

It's not only tourists who visit this excellent *Heurige* restaurant. The wines are bright and clean tasting and the buffet, while not outstanding, is good value. Live music and, of course, a garden.

Michl's Churrascaria 18

Nussdorferpl. 8	
℘ 370 6237	
🚇 U-Bahn Nussdorf	
Open: Mon–Sat 1800–2400, Sun 1200–1430	
Reservations unnecessary	
All credit cards accepted	
Brazilian	
ⓖⓖ	

This increasingly popular Latin American outfit specialises in Brazilian spit roasts and banana fritters. The philosophy is simple: pay once and eat as much as you can. Garden seating.

Plachutta 19

Heiligenstädterstr. 179	
℘ 370 4125	

🔵 Tram D

Open: daily 1130–2230	
Reservations unnecessary	
All credit cards accepted	
Austrian	
🔵🔵	

There are currently three branches of this popular chain of restaurants. The atmosphere is a bit subdued, almost staid, but the prime cuts of melt-in-the-mouth Styrian beef keep the attention of most customers firmly focused on the food. The wines too are good value, or there's the feisty Hietzinger beer. Moderate-sized garden.

Rudolfshof 🔵20

Cobenzlg. 8	
✆ 322 108	
🔵 Bus 38A	
Open: daily 1300–2300	
Reservations unnecessary	
All credit cards accepted	
Viennese	
🔵🔵–🔵🔵🔵	

Enjoy typical Viennese *Hausmannskost* (buffet or à la carte) while sitting in the shady garden. Live performances of traditional *Schrammelmusik* (accordion) start around 1800.

Weingut Reinprecht 🔵21

Cobenzlg. 22	
✆ 320 14710	
🔵 Bus 38A	
Open: Mar–Nov daily 1530–2400	
Reservations unnecessary	
All credit cards accepted	
Viennese	
🔵🔵🔵	

The prize-winning Veltliner wines are enough of an excuse to visit this outstanding *Heurige* with a large garden stretching towards the Weinberg. You could spend hours hovering over the extensive, self-service buffet and there's entertainment in the form of traditional Viennese music.

Weinschlössl 🔵22

Grinzingerallee 78	
✆ 320 6912	
🔵 Tram 38	

Open: Mon–Fri 1800–2400, Sat–Sun 1130–2400	
Reservations recommended	
All credit cards accepted	
Viennese	
🔵🔵🔵	

The first operetta *Heurige* in Vienna (or so they claim!). For a reasonable price you get a five-course meal, a bottle of wine and admission to the show. Sing along to excerpts from *Die Fledermaus*, *The Gypsy Baron* and *The Merry Widow* and classics by Johann Strauss, Franz Léhar, and others.

▲ Weingut Reinprecht

GRINZING
Bars, cafés and pubs

Anton Huber

Sieveringstr. 141

∅ 320 1473

🚌 Bus 39A

Open: Mon–Fri 0900–0200, Sat 1500–0200, Sun 1800–0200

❻–❻❻

A typical neighbourhood café serving a limited range of traditional Austrian dishes throughout the day. Austrian and international newspapers are available and there's a small garden.

Aristo ㉔

Grinzingerstr. 70

∅ 370 5283

🚌 Bus 38A

Open: daily 2100–0400

❻

Renowned physicist Albert Einstein once lived on the premises of this late-night café-bar. It sells snacks as well as cocktails and sparkling wines. Takes all credit cards.

Fuji ㉕

Grinzingerstr. 72

∅ 378 0668

🚌 Bus 38A

Open: daily 1130–1500, 1730–2300

❻❻

Sushi bar (part of a chain) with a picture menu in English and Japanese. The raw fish and shellfish combinations include tuna, mackerel, eel, crab, sweet shrimp, clam, scallop, squid, tuna, red snapper and sea bass.

Grinzinger Stüberl ㉖

Helga-Hängelpl. 19/Sandg. 7

∅ None available

🚌 Bus 38A

Open: daily 2000–0200

❻

Lokal in central Grinzing selling coffee and snacks – soups, toast, and so on.

Martin-Sepp Beisl im Trummelhof ㉗

Cobenzlg. 30

∅ 320 32334/0669 3232333

🚌 Bus 38A

Open: daily 1900–2400

❻–❻❻

More of a snack-bar than a *Beisl* – if you want a full meal the Martin Sepp *Heurige* is next door. It sells draught beer and *gespritzer* wine. The Romanesque foundations of the 19th-century building belong to the 'Trummel' tower – part of an ancient castle.

Nussdorfer Bräustüberl ㉘

Heiligenstädterstr. 205b

∅ 370 2107

🚋 Tram D

Open: Mon–Sat 1600–2300, Sun 1130–2300

❻❻

Austria's smallest brewery dispenses five robust, home-produced beers. You can also sample the hearty home cooking. Large garden and several back rooms.

Rudolf Tendshert ㉙

Cobenzlg. 6

∅ 322 108

🚌 Bus 38A

Open: daily 1000–2300

❻

Café-Konditorei next door to **Rudolfshof** (*see page 83*). Sells the famous Sachertorte, as well as its own brand of cake.

Shakes & Beer ㉚

Nussdorferpl. 5

∅ 370 1202

🚇 U-Bahn Nussdorf or tram D

Open: summer daily 1830–0100; winter daily 1000–0100

❻

Café-pub offering cheap snacks and draught Guinness. Cosy back room with open fireplace.

GRINZING
Shops, markets and picnic sites

Bakeries

Bäckerei Holzer ③①

Himmelstr. 21

🚋 Tram 38

Open: Mon–Fri 0530–1830, Sat 0530–1200

Holzer is a *Café-Konditorei* as well as a bakery. Sandwiches, sausage rolls and drinks for sale.

Fronza Gelatomania ③②

Grinzingerstr. 145

🚌 Bus 38A

Open: Mar–Sep daily 0930–2300

As well as 20 different flavours of ice cream, you can also buy light breakfast, desserts and coffee. Air-conditioned rooms and a terrace.

Nahodil ③③

Sieveringerstr. 4–10

🚋 Tram 38

Open: daily 0700–2100

Cake shop and café serving breakfasts from 0700 to 1100 and hot dishes from 1100 to 1500.

Nöbauer ③④

Himmelstr. 7

🚋 Tram 38

Open: daily 0800–1900

Small cake shop with plenty of seating, both inside and out.

Grocers and supermarkets

Aibler ③⑤

Heiligenstädterstr. 183

🚌 Bus 38A

Open: Mon–Fri 0800–1830, Sat 0800–1300

Delicatessen with a good line in strudels, as well as cheeses, salads and grilled chicken.

Nussdorfer Markt ③⑥

Heiligenstädterstr.

🚋 Tram D

You'll find this small parade of shops on the road leading from Nussdorf to Heiligenstadt. *Stands 2–3*: Excellent fruit and vegetable store: strawberries, farm tomatoes, mushrooms, figs, chestnuts, and so on. *Stand 4*: Small Feinkost supermarket with bakery counter. *Stand 4*: Beer parlour and snack bar, dishing up soups and *Würzel*. Eat in or take away. *Stand 5*: Al Bakhri, a shop specialising in Middle Eastern/Turkish edibles, including houmous, taramasalata, cheeses, oriental breads, *halva*, olive oils and olives. *Stand 6*: Poultry shop with delicatessen counter and *rôtisserie*.

Rudolf Tendshert ③⑦

Cobenzlg. 8

🚌 Bus 38A

Open: Mon–Fri 0730–1900, Sat 0730–1300

Well-stocked delicatessen with *rôtisserie* and simple dishes of the day.

Picnic sites

Heiligenstadt Park ③⑧

🚌 Bus 38A

Just beyond St Michael's Church in Heiligenstadt you'll find a small park with a few benches, a children's playground and tennis courts.

▲ *Topfenstrudel*

Heurige

Gastronomic delights

Vines have flourished on the sunny slopes of the Nussberg, Bisamberg and Lauerberg for hundreds of years. So much wine was produced that, according to legend, the mortar that binds the Stephansdom together was mixed using the surplus. Even today, despite the encroaching suburbs, there are 700 hectares under cultivation.

Heurige are the picturesque rural inns that sell the current year's (*heuer*) wine from their own vineyards (a privilege granted by Joseph II in the 18th century). When the new vintage is ready for drinking a bunch of fir twigs is hung by the gate alongside a sign with the word 'Ausg'steckt'. *Heurige* wines are made from different varieties of white grape planted, harvested and vinified together (*gemischter Satz*). A true *Weinbeisser* (connoisseur) will have no problem identifying the full-bodied wines of Grinzing and Heiligenstadt, the more acidic strains from Neustift and Sievering and the fruitier varieties of Stammersdorf.

In the typical *Heurige* food and wine go hand in hand. The buffet counter heaves with roast meats, cheeses, pastries, salads and desserts. You can also sample the plain home cooking known as 'Hausmannskost' – black pudding, liver sausage, crackling, knuckle of pork, *Aufläufe* (a soufflé of meat, sausage and potatoes or noodles) or strudels filled with meat or vegetables.

No *Heurige* experience is complete without *Schrammelmusik*. 'Invented' by the Schrammel brothers in the 19th century, these folk medleys on fiddle, accordion and guitar, sometimes with vocal accompaniment, are performed al fresco, in the garden or courtyard.

OPENING TIMES

Each *Heurige* has its own opening times. While a few stay open all year round, the season generally lasts from March until October. Check which inns are open before you set out. Note too that few *Heurige* open for lunch – people generally start arriving in the late afternoon or early evening.

• **Alt-Sievering** *Sieveringerstr. 63; ☎ 320 5888; ◉ tram 38; open: Thu-Mon 0900–2400; reservations recommended;* 🖭 ●; *Viennese;* ❶❷❸. This place has been around for more than 300 years. Walter Slupetzky and his family know the business inside out and it's a refreshing change to find vegetarian dishes on the otherwise typical menu.

• **Braunsperger** *Sieveringerstr. 108; ✆ 320 3992;* 🚋 *tram 38; open: every odd month, daily 1500–2400; reservations recommended; all credit cards accepted; Viennese;* ❻❻. This *Heurige*, on the fringes of Sievering, attracts fewer tourists than those on Grinzing high street. There's a good choice of desserts, as well as the usual hot and cold buffet, while the wines include Zweigelt and classic *gemischter Satz*.

... picturesque rural inns that sell the current year's wine from their own vineyards ...

• **Eckel** *Sieveringerstr. 46; ✆ 320 3218;* 🚋 *tram 38; open: Tue–Sat 1200–1430, 1800–2230; reservations recommended; all credit cards accepted; Viennese;* ❻❻. This excellent garden restaurant deserves praise for the quality and affordability of its homely Viennese dishes.

• **Karl Berger** *Himmelstr. 19; ✆ 320 5893;* 🚌 *bus 38A; open: Easter–Oct daily 1600–2400; reservations unnecessary; all credit cards accepted; Viennese;* ❻❻. A family-run *Heurige* with comfortable, old-fashioned parlours and a delightful courtyard. The buffet features homemade specialities, while the wines include several prizewinners.

• **Kierlinger** *Kahlenbergerstr. 20; ✆ 370 2264;* 🚋 *U-Bahn Nussdorf, then taxi; open: daily 1530–2400; reservations recommended; all credit cards accepted; Viennese;* ❻❻❻. One of the best *Heurige* restaurants in Vienna. Wines have been cultivated on this part of the Nussberg since the 18th century and the Rhein-Rieslings and Traminers are still winning medals. The cooking too is excellent value and children are welcome to roam in the extensive, well-shaded garden.

• **Mandahus** *Greinerg. 29; ✆ 370 4679;* 🚋 *tram D; open: daily 1600–2300; reservations recommended; all credit cards accepted; Viennese;* ❻❻. The garden is the big plus at this attractive *Heurige* but the buffet is uninspired and the wines undistinguished. Nevertheless, people seem to have a good time.

• **Schübel-Auer** *Kahlenbergerstr. 22; ✆ 370 2222;* 🚋 *U-Bahn Nussdorf, then taxi; open: Mon–Sat 1600–2400; reservations recommended; all credit cards accepted; Viennese;* ❻❻. It's the *Schrammelmusik* that provides this Nussdorf *Heurige* with a loyal band of regular customers. The buffet is extensive, with a large selection of cheeses and some vegetarian alternatives. Large garden.

• **Steinschaden** *Kahlenbergerstr. 18; ✆ 370 1375;* 🚋 *U-Bahn Nussdorf, then taxi; open: Mon–Fri 1500–2400, Sat 1430–2400, Sun 1430–2200; reservations recommended; all credit cards accepted; Viennese;* ❻❻. *Heurige* restaurant with a playing area for children in the garden. Warm and cold buffet, excellent homegrown wines and a mouthwatering selection of strudels.

Food etiquette and culture

WHERE TO EAT

Many of Vienna's best cafés and restaurants lie conveniently within the confines of the Innen Stadt, the historic inner city. As the streets here, especially around the Stephansdom, are pedestrianised, looking for somewhere to eat can itself be a pleasurable experience.

While culinary standards (and price levels) are set by the luxury hotels, which can command the services of superb chefs such as Reinhard Gerer – a renowned exponent of Austrian **nouvelle cuisine** – it's not necessary to burn a hole in your pocket to enjoy an excellent meal. Some of the most interesting restaurants offer **regional specialities** from Styria, Carinthia or the Tyrol – a reminder that Austrian cooking is a true hybrid, drawing on Hungarian, Bohemian, Slav and Italian influences. The number of **ethnic restaurants** showcasing cuisines from all over the world is on the increase – dominating the field at the moment are the

Italians (Tuscan cooking is especially popular) and the Japanese.

For an **informal meal** in a relaxed setting you can't beat the *Beisl*. A cross between an English pub and a French bistro, this Austrian institution comes into its own at lunchtime when each *Lokal* attracts its own regular clientele. Predictions that the growth in fast-food outlets and ethnic cafés would lead to its demise, or at least decline, have proved unfounded. *Beisln* specialise in *Hausmannskost*, nourishing no-frills home cooking.

Both the *Kaffeehaus* and the *Café-Konditorei* (*pâtisserie*) serve not only the cakes and pastries for which Austria is famous the world over but mouth-watering varieties of open sandwiches. If you're shopping for a picnic, the *Konditorei* is a good port of call; alternatively, try a local delicatessen or bakery. Some of the best delicatessens are in large supermarkets such as Julius Meinl. If you want to eat on the go Austrian style, then buy a *Frankfurter* or *Debreziner* (Hungarian sausage) from a *Wurstelstand*.

WHEN TO EAT

In Austria **breakfast** (served from around 0800 in some places) is a light affair of crusty bread rolls (*Semmeln*) and coffee. It's followed at around 1000 by

Gabelfrühstück (literally 'fork breakfast'), an altogether weightier combination of meat hash, sausages, goulash, eggs, black pudding and fried offal, washed down with a glass of *Nuss* (wine from Wiener Nussberg). **Lunch** (*Mittagessen*) is the main meal of the day, served from around 1200. Similar to the English tradition of **afternoon tea** is the Austrian *Jause* (pause for coffee and cakes). **Dinner** (*Abendessen*) usually begins at around 1800, while kitchens close at approximately 2300. That said, late-night eating is becoming increasingly fashionable.

If you want to eat in a particular restaurant, be sure to book and note that coffeehouses do not accept **reservations**. Bear in mind too that many establishments close for several weeks in July and August and again around January, so check before you set out.

HOW TO ORDER

While a knowledge of German is still useful in deciphering the menu, English is widely spoken and translations are often available. Main courses usually arrive with servings of vegetables and dumplings, but side salads should be ordered separately. A small charge is usually made for bread. If you're drinking wine with your meal, consider ordering by the glass as it often works out cheaper. Ask for *ein Achtel* if you want a small glass or *ein Viertel*. If you like mineral water, Austrian Voslauer is one of the world's leading brands.

Service is often included in the bill but a tip of about 10 per

cent is customary. Computerised bills are now commonplace; in *Beisln*, however, the waiter will tot up the amount on the spot. Credit cards are widely accepted but take cash if you intend to eat in a *Beisl*.

Most Viennese restaurants welcome **children** and offer half portions but rarely special menus. So if it's a burger and chips they're after, head for the nearest fast-food outlet. Few restaurants operate a no-smoking policy – the best you can hope for is a non-smoking table in a designated area. **Wrenkh** and **Siddhartha** are among a handful of restaurants catering specifically for **vegetarians**, otherwise it's a good idea to state at the outset '*Ich bin Vegetarianer*' (I am a vegetarian).

Menu decoder

GENERAL TERMS
Beilagen – extras/side dishes
Getränke inbegriffen – drinks
  included
Hauptgericht – main course
hausgemacht – homemade
kalte Speisen – cold main
  courses
Nachspeisen – desserts
Spezialitäten – house specialities
Tagesmenü – dish/menu of the
  day
Tellergerichte – one-course meals
Vorspeisen – appetisers
warme Vorgerichte – hot
  appetisers
Zuschlag – additional charge

COOKING METHODS
blutig – rare
fertige Speisen – ready cooked
gebraten – roasted
gebacken – fried
gedämpft – steamed
gedünstet – braised
gegrillt – grilled
gekocht – boiled
geschwenkt – sautéed
geschmort – stewed
gut durchgebraten – well done
mittel – medium
paniert – breaded
pochiert – poached
roh – raw

APPETISERS
Eintopf – stew
Griesknockerlsuppe – soup made
  with semolina dumplings
Gulaschsuppe – goulash soup
Hühnersuppe – chicken soup
Kürbiskremsuppe – Styrian soup
made with pumpkins
serbische Bohnensuppe – Serbian
  bean soup
Schwammerlsuppe – delicious
  speciality soup made with
  mushrooms
Tagessuppe – soup of the day

SIDE DISHES
Eierschwammerl – Chanterelle
  mushrooms served with salad
gekochtes Ei – boiled egg
Kartoffelsalat – potato salad
Krapfen/Kucherl – fritters
Jägersalat – literally 'hunter's
  salad', made from Chinese
  cabbage
Knödel – dumplings made with
  bread or potatoes
Nockerln – Austrian version of
  pasta
Nudel – noodles
Pommes frittes – French fries,
  chips
Reis – rice
Rühreier – scrambled eggs
Salat – salad
Spätzle – egg noodles
Spiegelei – fried eggs

HERBS, PULSES AND VEGETABLES
Blattsalat – lettuce
Bohnen – beans
Champignons – button
  mushrooms
Eierschwammerl – mushrooms
Erbsen – peas
Fisolen – green beans
Gurke – cucumber
Karfiol – cauliflower
Karotten – carrots

Kartoffel – potatoes
Knoblauch – garlic
Lauch – leek
Mais – corn on the cob
Paprika – pepper (green/red/yellow)
rote Beete – beetroot
Rotkohl/Rotkraut – red cabbage
Sauerkraut – pickled cabbage
Spargel – asparagus
Zwiebel – onions

MEAT, POULTRY AND GAME
Backhendl – chicken fried in breadcrumbs
Bauernschmaus – hefty platter of hot meats, comprising ham, sausage, roast pork and smoked cuts, usually served with dumplings and sauerkraut
Beuschl – heart and lung of beef in a rich, piquant sauce, often accompanied by a single giant dumpling
Blunzn – black pudding
Čevapčiči – Serbian meat rissoles
Debreziner – fatty Hungarian sausage flavoured with spicy paprika
Gulasch – meat stew, spiced with paprika
Hühn(er) – chicken
Jungfernbraten – loin of pork
Kalb – veal
Karree – smoked shoulder of pork
Krenfleisch – boiled pork with grated horseradish

Lamm – lamb
Leber – liver
Puter/Truthahn – turkey
Rind(fleisch) – beef
Rostbraten – roast or pan-fried sirloin
Schinken – ham
Schwein – pork
Speck – bacon
Stelze – classic Viennese dish, comprising shin of pork with bread dumplings, cabbage salad and horseradish
Tafelspitz – boiled silverside of beef, thickly sliced and served with roast or fried grated potatoes and apple and horseradish sauce (Kren)
Vanillerostbraten – beef with garlic seasoning
Wiener Schnitzel – breaded veal

or pork escalope, deep-fried until golden, served with slice of lemon

Wurst – sausage

Zwiebelrostbraten – beefsteak served with crispy fried onions

FISH

Austern – oysters
Forelle – trout
Garnelen – prawns
Hummer – lobster
Kabeljau – cod
Karpfen – carp
Krabbe – crab
Lachs – salmon
Matjes – herring
Muscheln – mussels
Seezunge – sole
Steinbutt – turbot
Tintenfisch – squid/cuttlefish
Thunfisch – tuna

DESSERTS

Mehlspeise – pudding
Torten – cakes, gateaux
Auflauf – soufflé
Buchteln – yeast dumplings, usually filled with jam or vanilla sauce
Eis – ice cream
Gebäck – pastry
Golatsche – puff-pastry envelope filled with sweet cream cheese
Gugelhupf – baked sponge cake with chocolate or, more usually, coffee flavouring
Kaiserschmarrn – omelette with raisins and compote of plums
Käse – cheese
Königskuchen – rum-flavoured loaf cake with almonds, raisins and currants
Krapfen – doughnuts
Kuchen – cakes, tarts, pastries
Linzertorte – jam tart with almond-flavoured pastry

Mohr im Hemd – 'Moor in a shirt', steamed chocolate pudding with nuts and ice cream

Mohrenkopf – 'Moor's Head', dome-shaped cake filled with custard or chilled whipped cream, flavoured with vanilla sugar, covered with hardened chocolate and served with a hot chocolate sauce

Palatschinken – pancakes filled with fruit, curd cheese, chocolate sauce or jam

Reisauflauf mit Äpfeln – rich rice soufflé, sometimes served with apple and raspberry syrup

Sahne – cream, plain or whipped (more commonly known as *Schlag* in Austria)

Salzburger Nockerl – sweet dough dumplings, poached in milk and served with hot vanilla sauce

Stollen – heavy cake with raisins, almonds, nuts and candied lemon peel

Strudel – flaky filo pastry wrapped around various fillings

Topfentascherl – envelope of curd cheese

Topfenknödel – curd cheese dumplings coated with breadcrumbs or ground walnuts, fried crisply in butter

FRUIT

Ananas – pineapple
Apfel – apple
Apfelsine/Orange– orange
Aprikosen/Marillen – apricots
Banane – banana
Birne – pear
Erdbeere – strawberry
Himbeere – raspberry
Kirsche – cherry

Pfirsich – peach
Rosine – raisin
Trauben – grapes
Zwetschge – plum

DRINKS
Bier – beer
Fruchtsaft – fruit juice
Gespritz – wine with mineral water
Glühwein – mulled wine
Kaffee – coffee
Milch – milk
Sekt – sparkling wine
Tee – tea
Wasser – water
Wein rot/weiss/schaum – wine red/white/sparkling

COFFEES
Einspänner – espresso coffee served in a glass with whipped cream
Eiskaffee – vanilla ice served in a glass with cold espresso and whipped cream
Fiaker – espresso with rum or brandy, served in a glass
Grosser/kleiner Brauner – large/small white coffee
Grosser/kleiner Schwarzer – large/small black coffee
Johann Strauss – large espresso with whipped cream and apricot
Kapuziner – cappuccino
Maria Theresia – espresso with orange liqueur, cream and sugar
Melange – coffee with a froth of milk and cream and a coating of chocolate powder
Mokka – black coffee, espresso

Recipes

Tafelspitz

Serves 4

INGREDIENTS

600g beef (topside)

50g ox liver

2 beef bones (150g)

1 carrot

1 parsnip

1 stick of celery

1 leek

1 clove of garlic

2 onions

1½ litres water

1 bay leaf

salt

5 peppercorns

nutmeg and parsley for garnish

Sauce:

2 medium apples

2 tbsp wine vinegar

3 tbsp grated horseradish

1–2 tsp sugar

salt

pepper

Rinse the bones, place them in a large saucepan and cover with cold water. Bring to the boil and skim – repeat this several times over. Add the meat, ox liver and roughly chopped vegetables. Skim again, then add the seasoning and simmer for 1 to 2 hours until tender.

While the meat is cooking, peel and grate the apples. Cook with the vinegar and sugar over a low heat for 12 minutes. Allow to cool, then stir in the grated horseradish.

▲ Tafelspitz

To serve:
Slice the beef on to a serving plate. Strain the stock, add nutmeg and salt to taste and pour a little over the meat. Sprinkle with chopped parsley and serve with the apple-horseradish sauce and fried potatoes.

Mohr im Hemd

Serves 4

INGREDIENTS

100g butter
100g sugar
6 eggs separated
100g grated cooking chocolate
100g grated almonds
100g breadcrumbs
butter and sugar to line the bowl

Chocolate sauce:

100g cooking chocolate
100g sugar
200ml water
250ml fresh cream

Beat the butter with the egg yolks and half the sugar until the mixture is light and fluffy. In a separate bowl mix the grated chocolate, almonds and bread-crumbs. Whisk the egg whites until stiff, then beat in the remainder of the sugar.

Fold alternate spoonfuls of the dry ingredients and beaten egg whites into the butter mixture, then spoon into a bowl which has been lightly greased and sprinkled with sugar. Cover and steam in a double-boiler for 1 hour. Allow to cool, then turn out on to a plate.

To make the sauce, boil the chocolate, sugar and water and stir well. Cook for 5 minutes, then pour over the pudding. Serve with whipped cream.

Published by Thomas Cook Publishing
Thomas Cook Holdings Ltd
PO Box 227
Thorpe Wood
Peterborough PE3 6PU
United Kingdom

Telephone: 01733 503571
Email: books@thomascook.com

Text © 2001 Thomas Cook Publishing
Maps © 2001 Thomas Cook Publishing

ISBN 1 841570 93 1

Distributed in the United States of
America by the Globe Pequot Press,
PO Box 480, Guilford, Connecticut
06437, USA

Publisher: Donald Greig
Commissioning Editor: Deborah Parker
Map Editor: Bernard Horton

Project management: Dial House
    Publishing
Series Editor: Christopher Catling
Copy Editor: Lucy Thomson
Proofreader: Jan Wiltshire

Series and cover design: WhiteLight
Cover artwork: WhiteLight and
    Kaarin Wall
Text layout: SJM Design Consultancy,
    Dial House Publishing
Maps prepared by Polly Senior
    Cartography

Repro and image setting: PDQ Digital
    Media Solutions Ltd
Printed and bound in Italy by
    Eurografica SpA

Written and researched by: **Chris and
    Melanie Rice**

The authors would like to give warm
thanks to Barbara Gigler and the staff of
the Austrian Tourist Board.

We would like to thank Ethel Davies for
the photographs used in this book, to
whom the copyright belongs, with the
exception of that on page 95: Neil
Setchfield.